ALAN DUNN'S

TROPICAL & EXOTIC FLOWERS

for Cakes

NEW HOLLAND

First published in 2011 by
New Holland Publishers (UK) Ltd
London · Cape Town · Sydney · Auckland

Garfield House
86–88 Edgware Road
London W2 2EA
United Kingdom

80 McKenzie Street
Cape Town 8001
South Africa

Unit 1
66 Gibbes Street
Chatswood
NSW 2067
Australia

218 Lake Road
Northcote
Auckland
New Zealand

ISBN 978 1 84773 868 4

Senior Editor: Lisa John
Photography: Sue Atkinson
Production: Laurence Poos
Design: Lucy Parissi
Publisher: Clare Sayer

2 4 6 8 10 9 7 5 3 1

Reproduction by PDQ Digital Media Solutions Ltd, United Kingdom
Printed and bound by Craft Print International Ltd, Singapore

Dedicated, and thank you, to the following tropical, exotic and native wildflowers: Tombi Peck, Alice Christie, Andrew Lockey, Christine Giles, Janet Seth, Norma Laver, Jenny Walker, Beverley Dutton, John Quai Hoi, Jay Aston, Joni Mitchell, Allen and Avril Dunn, Susan and Mark Laird, Sathyavathi Narayanswamy, Lisa John and finally to Sue Atkinson for her wonderful reflective photography!

Contents

Introduction

It is now almost twenty-five years since I started cake decorating and making sugar flowers. The first flowers I was taught were the rose, carnation and sweet-pea – all flowers that I loved making. However, it was the lessons that followed on exotic orchids and other more exotic and tropical flowers that really captured my imagination and fuelled my passion for making flowers.

I have included several exotic flowers in most of my previous books but I was thrilled to be given the chance to write this book concentrating on some of my more favourite tropical and exotic flowers and foliage. This book features many familiar exotic flowers as well as some more unusual species, combining them to create eye-catching displays that work well on all types of celebration cakes.

I love working with strong and vibrantly coloured flowers, foliage, berries and seed-heads, often using what seem like clashing colours at first glance but trying to strike a colour note that helps create a happy balance to make them 'sing' together. With the cakes and floral displays in this book I have tried to illustrate how the flowers can be used in a way that would appeal to the general public and cake decorators alike. It can sometimes be tricky introducing unusual and exotic flowers into cake design and sometimes the inclusion of the ever-popular and more familiar rose is all that is needed to convince a customer or recipient that tropical and exotic

flowers can help add extra interest and drama to a cake design.

Whenever I travel I try to take photographs and sketches of the flowers I see, dissecting them to make templates, which always comes in very useful when I get home to start work on creating those flowers in sugar or cold porcelain.It is also fairly easy to obtain many species from garden centres and from florists. I also have a large collection of flower and gardening books, which can make reference work much easier, as well as images and a whole load of information at my disposal on the internet.

How closely you copy the flowers will depend on how you intend to use them. For a competition, you will need them to be fairly accurate. If you are creating flowers for you or a cake commission, however, don't be afraid to alter and tweak the flowers to create something that might not be botanically correct but captures the spirit of the plant or reflects the mood that you yourself are in at the time of creating them. Go with your gut instinct and enjoy what can often be a fairly time-consuming process. This is what makes the work unique and adds character to a display. The cakes and floral displays in this book are there only as suggestions and you can decide to recreate them exactly or mix and match the elements to create designs individual to you.

Alan Dunn

EQUIPMENT, MATERIALS, RECIPES AND TECHNIQUES

There is a huge array of sugarcraft equipment and materials available commerically. Here, a variety of items that I consider to be very useful are listed.

EQUIPMENT

Non-stick board

This is an essential addition to the flower-maker's workbox. Avoid white boards as they strain the eyes too much. Some boards can be very shiny, making it difficult to frill the petals against them. If this is the case, simply roughen up the surface using some fine glass paper prior to use or turn over the board and use the back, which is often less shiny. I always apply a thin layer of white vegetable fat rubbed into the surface of the board, then remove most of the excess with dry kitchen paper – this stops the paste sticking to the board and also makes you check each time to see if it is clean from food colour.

Rolling pins

It's good to have a selection of non-stick rolling pins in various sizes. They are essential for rolling out flowerpaste, sugarpaste and almond paste successfully.

Foam pads

Foam pads are ideal to place petals and leaves on while you soften the edges. Make sure you buy one with a good surface as some have a rough-textured surface that will tear the edges of your petals or leave marks on them. I prefer either the large blue pad called a Billy's block or the yellow celpad.

Wires and floristry tape

I buy mostly white paper-covered wires, preferring to colour or tape over as I work. The most consistent wires for quality are the Japanese Sunrise wires. These are available from 35-gauge (very fine but rare) to 18-gauge (thicker). Floristry tape is used in the construction of stems and bouquets. It contains a glue that is released when the tape is stretched. I use mainly Lion Brand nile green, brown and white tape.

Tape shredder

This tool contains three razor blades to cut floristry tape into quarter-widths. I have a couple of tape shredders and have removed two blades from one of them so that it cuts the tape into half-widths. Tape can often stick to an excess of glue left behind on the blades – rubbing a tiny amount of cold cream onto the blades with a cotton bud and also a little onto the lid that presses against the blades will help the tape run smoothly. It is also wise to remove any build-up of glue from the blades using fine-nose pliers and also to replace the blades regularly. Handle with care at all times.

Paintbrushes and dusting brushes

Good-quality, synthetic brushes or synthetic-blend brushes from art shops are best for flower-making. I use mainly short, flat, not too soft bristle brushes for applying layers of food colour dusts. To avoid having to wash them so regularly, it is best to keep brushes for certain colours. I use finer sable or synthetic-blend brushes for painting fine lines or detail spots onto petals.

Petal, flower and leaf cutters and veiners

There is a huge selection of cutters available from cake decorating shops, both in metal and plastic. There is also an impressive selection of commercial petal and leaf

HOMEMADE LEAF/PETAL VEINERS

There are several craft products available that can be used to make moulds for leaves, petals, fruit, nuts and so on. It is important to try to find a food-grade product. Silicone plastique is a good medium to use with a quick-drying time. When making a mould of a petal or leaf, it is important to choose items with prominent veins. Note that most flowers and foliage produce stronger veins as they age. To make a mould:

1 Silicone plastique can be purchased as a kit. Mix the two compounds together thoroughly. The white material is the base and the blue is the catalyst – once mixed you will have about 10–20 minutes of working time before the medium sets – this often depends on the room temperature. It is important to flatten the product onto a sheet of plastic wrap or a plastic food bag as it tends to stick to everything in its sight.

2 Press the back of your chosen leaf or petal into the silicone putty, taking care to press the surface evenly to avoid air bubbles, which will create a fault in the veiner. When the compound has set, simply peel off the leaf or petal. Trim away any excess silicone from around the mould using a pair of scissors.

3 Next, very lightly grease the leaf veiner with cold cream cleanser – be careful not to block up the veins with the cream as this will ruin the final result. Mix up another amount of the two compounds and press firmly on top of the first half of the leaf veiner, again taking care to press evenly. When the second half has set, pull the two sides apart: you now have a double-sided leaf veiner.

moulds/veiners to choose from. These are made from food-grade silicone rubber. They are useful for creating natural petal and leaf texturing for sugar work.

Posy picks

These are used to hold the handle of a spray or bouquet of flowers in a cake. They come in various sizes and are made from food-grade plastic, which protects the cake from contamination by wires and floristry tape. Never push wires directly into a cake.

Stamens and thread

There is a huge selection of commercial stamens available from cake decorating shops. I use mainly fine white and seed-head stamens, which I can then colour using powder colours. Fine cotton thread is best for stamens. I use lace-making Brock 120 white thread, although thicker threads may be useful for larger flowers. An emery board is great for fluffing up the tips of the thread to form anthers.

Glue

Non-toxic glue sticks can be bought from stationery or art shops and are great for fixing ribbon to the cake drum's edge. Always make sure that the glue does not come into direct contact with the cake. I use a hi-tack, non-toxic craft glue to attach stamens to the end of wires. The glue should not come into direct contact with the sugar petals as it will dissolve them.

Scissors, pliers, wire cutters and tweezers

Fine embroidery and curved scissors are very useful for cutting fine petals, thread and ribbons too. Larger florist's scissors are useful for cutting wires and ribbon. Small, fine-nose pliers are another essential. Good-quality pliers from electrical supply shops are best – they are expensive but well worth the investment. Electrical wire cutters are useful for cutting heavier wires. It is important to use fine, angled tweezers without ridges (or teeth). They are useful for pinching ridges on petals and holding very fine petals and stamens. They are also handy when arranging flowers to push smaller items into difficult, tight areas of an arrangement or spray.

Plain-edge cutting wheel (PME) and scalpel

This is rather like a small double-sided pizza wheel. It is great for cutting out quick petals and leaves, and also for adding division lines to buds. A scalpel is essential for marking veins, adding texture and cutting out petal shapes too.

Metal ball tools (CC/Celcakes)

I use mostly metal ball tools to work the edges of petals and leaves. These are heavier than plastic ball tools, which means that less effort is needed to soften the paste. I mostly work the tool using a rubbing or rolling action against the paste, positioning it half on the petal/leaf edge and half on my hand or foam pad that the petal is resting against. It can also be used to 'cup' or hollow out petals to form interesting shapes.

Dresden/veining tool (J or PME)

The fine end of this tool is great for adding central veins to petals or leaves, and the broader end can be used for working the edges of a leaf to give a serrated effect or a 'double-frilled' effect on the edges of petals. Simply press the tool against the paste repeatedly to create a tight frilled effect or pull the tool against the paste on a non-stick board to create serrations. The fine end of the tool can also be used to cut into the edge of the paste to cut and flick finer serrated-edged leaves. I use a black tool by Jem for finer, smaller leaves and flowers, and the larger yellow PME tool for larger flowers.

Ceramic tools (HP/Holly Products)

A smooth ceramic tool is used for curling the edges of petals and hollowing out throats of small flowers, as well as serving the purpose of a mini rolling pin. Another of the ceramic tools, known as the silk veining tool, is wonderful for creating delicate veins and frills to petal edges.

Celsticks (CC/Celcakes)

Celsticks come in four sizes and are ideal for rolling out small petals and leaves and to create thick ridges. The pointed end of the tool is great for opening up the centre of 'hat'-type flowers. The rounded end can be used in the same way as a ball tool, to soften edges and hollow out petals.

Kitchen paper ring formers

These are great for holding and supporting petals to create a cupped shape as they dry allowing the paste/petal to breathe, which speeds up the drying process (plastic formers tend to slow down the drying process). To make, cut a strip of kitchen paper diagonally in half, twist it back onto itself and then tie it in a loop, or for larger petals, cut a sheet of kitchen paper diagonally across, twist and tie.

MATERIALS

Egg white

You will need fresh egg white to stick petals together and to sometimes alter the consistency of the paste if it is too dry. Many cake decorators avoid the use of fresh egg white because of salmonella scares. I continue to use Lion brand eggs and always work with a fresh egg white each time I make flowers. There are commercially available edible glues that can be used instead of egg white but I find these tend to dissolve the sugar slightly before allowing it to dry, resulting in weak petals.

White vegetable fat

I use this to grease non-stick boards and then wipe of it off with dry kitchen paper. This conditions the board, helping prevent the flowerpaste sticking to it, and also removes any residual food colour. You can add a tiny amount of white fat to the paste if it is very sticky. You must be careful not to leave too much fat on the board as greasy patches will show up on the petals when you apply the dry dusting colours.

Cornflour bag

Cornflour is a life-saver when the flowerpaste is sticky. It is best to make a cornflour bag using disposable nappy liners. Fold a couple of layers of nappy liners together and add a good tablespoon of cornflour on top. Tie the nappy liner together into a bag using ribbon or an elastic band. This bag is then used to lightly dust the paste prior to rolling it out and also on petals/leaves before they are placed into a veiner.

Petal dusts

These food colour dusts contain a gum that helps them to adhere to the petal or leaf. They are wonderful for creating very soft and also very intense colouring to finished flowers. The dusts can be mixed together to form different colours or brushed on in layers, which creates more interest and depth to the finished flower or leaf. White petal dust can be added to soften the colours. If you are trying to create bold, strong colours it is best to dust the surface of the flowerpaste while it is still fairly pliable or at the leather-hard stage. A paint can also be made by adding clear alcohol (isopropyl) to the dust. This is good for adding spots and finer details. This dust can also be added to melted cocoa butter to make a paint that is ideal for painting designs onto the surface of a cake. Petal dusts can be used in small amounts to colour flowerpaste to create interesting and subtle base colours.

Paste food colours

These give quite a strong colour. I add paste colours to sugarpaste to cover cakes but I am not a huge fan of strongly coloured cake coverings. It is best to mix up a small ball of sugarpaste with some paste food colour and then add this ball to a larger amount of paste – this way, you will avoid adding too much colour to the entire amount of sugarpaste.

Liquid colours

These are generally used to colour royal icing, as they alter the consistency of flowerpaste, sugarpaste and almond paste but they can also be great to paint with. I mostly use cyclamen and poinsettia red liquid colours to paint fine spots and fine lines to petals.

Craft dusts

These are inedible so only intended for items that are not going to be eaten. Craft dusts are much stronger and much more light-fast than food colour dusts. Care must be taken – dust in an enclosed space, as once these colours get into the air they have a habit of landing where you don't want them to.

Glazes and varnishes

See page 13.

RECIPES

COLD PORCELAIN

This is an inedible air-drying craft paste that can be used in almost exactly the same way as flowerpaste. The bonus with this paste is that the flowers made from it are much stronger and less prone to breakages. However, because it is inedible, anything made from this paste cannot come into direct contact with a cake's surface, so flowers made from cold porcelain need to be placed in a vase, container, candle-holder or Perspex plaque. I tend to treat flowers made with this paste pretty much as I would fresh or silk flowers. There are several commercial cold porcelain pastes available but you can make your own – the recipe below is the one that I prefer. I use measuring spoons and measuring cups to measure out the ingredients.

INGREDIENTS

2½ tbsp baby oil

115 ml (4 fl oz/½ cup) non-toxic hi-tack craft glue (Impex)

115 ml (4 fl oz/½ cup) white PVA wood glue (Liberon Super wood glue or Elmers)

125 g (4½ oz/1 cup) cornflour

Permanent white artist's gouache paint

1 Work in a well-ventilated area when making this paste. Wear a filter mask if you suffer from asthma. Measure the baby oil and the two glues together in a non-stick saucepan to form an emulsion. Stir the cornflour into the mixture. It will go lumpy at this stage but this is normal.

2 Place the pan over a medium heat and stir the paste with a heavy-duty plastic or wooden spoon. The paste will gradually come away from the base and sides of the pan to form a ball around the spoon. Scrape any uncooked paste from the spoon and add it to the mix. The cooking time – usually around 10 minutes – will vary between gas, electric and ceramic hobs, but the general rule is the lower the heat and the slower you mix the paste, the smoother the resulting paste will be. I'm impatient so I tend to turn up the heat a little to cook faster. Keep on stirring the paste to cook it evenly. You will need to split the paste and press the inner parts of the ball against the heat of the pan to cook it too – be careful not to overcook.

3 Turn the paste onto a non-stick board and knead until smooth. The paste is quite hot at this stage. The kneading should help distribute some heat through the paste to cook any undercooked areas. If the paste is very sticky then you will need to put it back in the pan to cook longer. It is better if it is slightly undercooked as you can always add heat later – if the paste is overcooked then it is almost impossible to work with.

4 Wrap in plastic wrap and leave to cool – moisture will build up on the surface of the paste that, if left, will encourage mould growth, so it is important to re-knead the paste when cool and then re-wrap. Place in a plastic food bag and then in an airtight container, and store at room temperature. This paste has been known to work well two years after it was made if stored like this.

5 Prior to making flowers you will need to add a smidge of permanent white gouache paint. The paste looks white but by its very nature dries clear, giving a translucence to the finished flower. Adding the paint makes the finish more opaque. Handling the paste is quite similar to working with sugar except I use cold cream cleanser instead of white vegetable fat, and glue or anti-bacterial wipes/water to moisten the petals to stick them. Cornflour is used as for handling flowerpaste. The paste shrinks a little as it dries – this is because of the glue. This can be disconcerting to begin with but you will gradually get used to it and it can be an advantage when making miniature flowers.

FLOWERPASTE

I always buy ready-made commercial flowerpaste (APOC) as it tends to be more consistent than homemade pastes. The following recipe is the one I used prior to discovering the joys of ready-made flowerpaste! Gum tragacanth gives the paste stretch and strength too.

INGREDIENTS

5 tsp cold water

2 tsp powdered gelatine

500 g (1 lb 2 oz/3 cups) icing sugar, sifted

3 tsp gum tragacanth

2 tsp liquid glucose

3 tsp white vegetable fat, plus 1 extra tsp to add later

1 large fresh egg white

1 Mix the cold water and gelatine together in a small bowl and leave to stand for 30 minutes. Sift the icing sugar and gum tragacanth together into the bowl of a heavy-duty mixer and fit to the machine.

2 Place the bowl with the gelatine mixture over a saucepan of hot water and stir until the gelatine has dissolved. Warm a teaspoon in hot water and then measure out the liquid glucose – the heat of the spoon should help to ease the glucose on its way. Add the glucose and 3 teaspoons of white vegetable fat to the gelatine mixture, and continue to heat until all the ingredients have dissolved and are thoroughly mixed together.

3 Add the dissolved gelatine mixture to the icing sugar/gum tragacanth with the egg white. Beat at the mixer's lowest speed, then gradually increase the speed to maximum until the paste is white and stringy.

4 Remove the paste from the bowl, knead into a smooth ball and cover with the remaining teaspoon of white vegetable fat – this helps to prevent the paste forming a dry crust that can leave hard bits in the paste at the rolling out stage. Place in a plastic food bag and store in an airtight container. Allow the paste to rest and mature for 12 hours before use.

5 The paste should be well-kneaded before you start to roll it out or model it into a flower shape, otherwise it has a tendency to dry out and crack around the edges. This is an air-drying paste so when you are not using it make sure it is well wrapped in a plastic bag. If you have cut out lots of petals, cover them over with a plastic bag.

TECHNIQUES

COATING A CAKE WITH ALMOND PASTE

I adore the flavour and texture of almond paste. A layer of natural-coloured white almond paste gives a smooth, round-edged base on which to apply a layer of sugarpaste, creating a more professional finish and excellent eating quality too! It is important that the work surface is free of flour or cornflour, as if any gets trapped between the almond paste and the sugarpaste it can cause fermentation, encouraging air bubbles. It is best, but not always essential, to leave the almond paste-coated cake to dry out and firm up for a few days prior to icing.

1 Before applying any form of coating, the cake must be level. To do this, carefully cut off the top of the cake if it has formed a dome during baking. Then turn the cake upside down so that the flat bottom becomes the top. Fill any large indentations with almond paste if required. Place the cake onto a thin cake board the same size as the cake so that it is easier to move. You might also prefer to add a strip of almond paste around the base of the cake to seal it and the cake board tightly together.

2 Warm some apricot jam and a dash of water, brandy or Cointreau, and then sieve to make an apricot glaze that can be painted onto the surface of the cake. This will help to stick the almond paste to the cake and help seal it to keep it fresh. Apricot glaze is used as the colour is not too dark and the flavour tends not to fight with the taste of the cake or almond paste. You may also be able to buy ready-sieved apricot glaze in a jar – which also benefits from a dash of alcohol.

3 You will need a long, non-stick rolling pin large enough to roll out almond paste to cover at least a 30 cm (12 in) cake. Plastic smoothers are also essential to create a professional finish: a curved smoother for the top of the cake and a square-edged one for the sides. Rolling out almond paste to an even thickness can be tricky, and a novice cake decorator might find a pair of marzipan spacers useful to roll against. Depending which way they are placed, they can produce thick or thin sheets of almond paste/sugarpaste. Store the paste in a warm place prior to kneading to help soften it slightly – otherwise it can be quite hard to work with. Knead the paste on a clean, dry surface to make it pliable.

4 Lightly dust the work surface with icing sugar. Place the almond paste on top and if needed position the spacers on either side of the paste. Roll the paste out lengthways using the non-stick rolling pin. Turn it sideways and reposition the spacers on either side again. Continue to roll out the paste until it is large enough to cover the cake. A measuring tape, string or even using the length of the rolling pin to gauge the exact size of the cake top and its sides can be useful. It is always best to allow slightly more than you think you will need, especially for awkward-shaped cakes or anything with corners to it.

5 Using a round-edged plastic smoother, polish and smooth out the surface of the almond paste. Start gently, gradually increasing the pressure to even out any slightly uneven areas of the paste.

6 Place the rolling pin on top of the almond paste and use it to help lift the paste over the cake. Remove the rolling pin and ease the almond paste into place. Smooth the surface of the cake to remove any air bubbles. Tuck the paste to fit the sides. If you are working on a cake with corners, it is best to concentrate on these first of all.

7 Use the curved-edge smoother to polish the top of the cake. Use strong, firm hand movements to 'iron out' any imperfections. Use the edge of the straight-edged smoother to cut and flick away the excess paste from the base of the cake. Finally, use the straight-edged smoother to iron out the sides of the cake using a fair amount of pressure. Place the cake onto a sheet of greaseproof paper and, if time allows, leave to firm up overnight or for a few days prior to coating with sugarpaste.

COATING A CAKE AND CAKE DRUM WITH SUGARPASTE

Plastic sugarpaste smoothers are essential when covering a cake with sugarpaste. The round-edged smoother is good for working on the top of the cake and the straight-edged smoother is good for working on the sides, giving a sharper edge at the base. Covering a cake with sugarpaste is a fairly straightforward process – however, practice is needed to achieve very neat results. If you are colouring the sugarpaste it is best to use paste food colour or to thicken liquid colours with icing sugar. It is safer to colour a small amount of sugarpaste and then knead this into the larger amount of paste to control the depth of colour rather than create a paste that is too brightly coloured.

1 Knead the sugarpaste on a clean, dry sugar- and flour-free surface until smooth and pliable. Try not to knead in too many air bubbles. When kneaded, lightly dust the work surface with sieved icing sugar and place the sugarpaste on top,

with any cracks against the work surface. Roll out, smooth and polish the paste as described for almond paste coating.

2 Moisten the surface of the almond paste with clear alcohol (Cointreau, kirsch or white rum can all be used). Use a sponge to apply the alcohol as this gives a more even covering. Any dry areas will encourage air bubbles to be trapped between the almond paste and the sugarpaste. The alcohol helps to stick the sugarpaste to the almond paste and also acts as an antibacterial agent.

WIRING PETALS AND LEAVES

This is my favourite method of constructing flowers. It gives the flowers much more movement and extra strength too, resulting in fewer breakages.

1 Knead a piece of flowerpaste and form roughly into the shape of the petal or leaf you are making. Press it down against a non-stick board to flatten it slightly. Use a celstick or rolling pin to roll the flowerpaste, leaving a ridge for the wire. Try to create a tapered ridge, angling the pin slightly so that the ridge is thicker at the base of the petal/leaf. The thickness and length of the ridge will depend on the size of the petal/leaf you are making. There are also boards available commercially, which have grooves in them that create a similar ridged effect when the paste is rolled over them. These can be great for smaller petals and leaves but I find that they produce too fine a ridge for many of the larger flowers that I make.

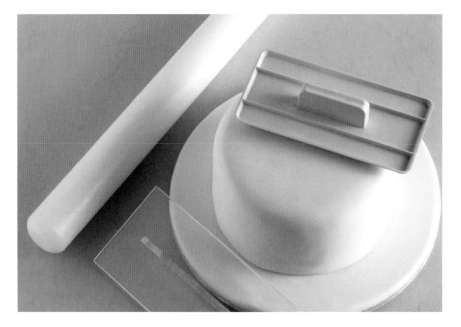

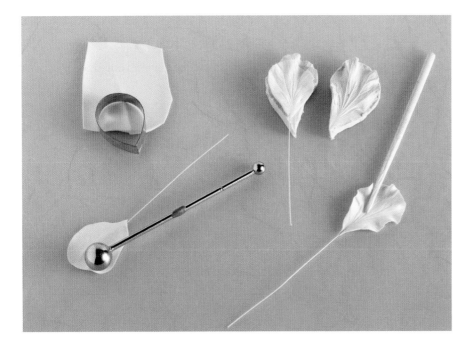

confectioners' varnish. This gives a very glossy finish but can be diluted with isopropyl alcohol (glaze cleaner/dipping solution) to give a lesser, more natural shine.

I use mainly a half-glaze – equal proportions of confectioners' varnish and alcohol as well as a ¼ glaze, which results in a very slight sheen, and a ¾ glaze, which gives a much stronger glaze. Mix the glaze and alcohol together in a clean jam jar. Do not shake as this will result in air bubbles in the glaze. Dip the leaves straight in the glaze and then shake off the excess glaze before hanging to dry or placing on kitchen paper to blot off any excess. The glaze can also be painted onto the leaf but I find the bristles of the brush create streaks.

Another method of glazing and setting the dry powder colour on leaves and petals is to hold the piece over a jet of steam from a just-boiled kettle or over a clothes steamer. Take care not to get the piece too wet in the steam and also be careful not to scald yourself. If you are trying to create a velvety effect on a flower or leaf, simply dust the colour onto the piece, steam and then re-dust. This is particularly good when making dark, rich red roses.

2 Cut out the petal/leaf shape using a cutter, scalpel or plain-edge cutting wheel, leaving the ridge to run down the centre. If you are using a cutter, lift up the shape and place it onto a very light dusting of cornflour and then press firmly with the cutter and scrub it slightly against the paste and the board so that the shape remains slightly stuck in the cutter. This will enable you to quickly rub the edge of the cutter to create a cleaner-cut edge, removing any fuzzy bits.

3 Moisten the wire very slightly – too much will result in the paper coming off the wire and also slow down the drying process of the petal on the wire. Hold the ridge firmly between your finger and thumb, and hold the wire in the other hand very close to the end of the wire that is being inserted into the shape. Push the wire in gradually so that it supports a third to half the length. Use a ball tool to soften and thin the edge of the shape using a rolling action, working the tool half on your hand/foam pad and half on the edge of the paste.

4 Place the petal/leaf into a double-sided petal/leaf veiner and press the two sides firmly against the shape to texture it.

5 A frilled edge can be added using a cocktail stick or a ceramic veining tool, working at intervals to encourage a natural frilled effect.

GLAZING AND STEAMING

There are several ways to glaze leaves, petals and berries. I favour the edible spray glaze made by Fabilo (APOC) as it is a much quicker process and creates a more efficient end result. This glaze may be used lightly for most leaves or in layers to create a stronger sheen for berries and glossy leaves. The alternative method is to use

TROPICAL AND EXOTIC CAKES, FLOWERS AND SPRAYS

Perfumed perfection

White perfume flowers form a stunning focal point to this beautiful cake design that would be wonderful as a small wedding or anniversary celebration cake. The delicate twisted petals of ylang-ylang flowers create lots of movement within the bouquet.

MATERIALS

25 cm (10 in) oval rich fruitcake placed on a thin cake board of the same size

35 cm (14 in) oval cake drum

1.25 kg (2 lb 12 oz) white almond paste

1.25 kg (2 lb 12 oz) white sugarpaste

Thin green and lemon striped ribbon

Clear alcohol (Cointreau or kirsch)

Broad pale lemon satin ribbon

Non-toxic glue stick

EQUIPMENT

Straight-edged and rounded-edged sugarpaste smoothers

Food-grade plastic posy pick

Fine-nose pliers

FLOWERS

Perfumed perfection bouquet (p 24)

1 Cover the cake and cake drum as described on pages 11–12. Allow to dry overnight. Transfer the cake centrally onto the drum and use the straight-edged sugarpaste smoother to blend the join between the base of the cake and the drum together. Next, polish the surface of the cake using a pad of sugarpaste pressed into your palm.

2 Attach a band of thin green and lemon striped ribbon around the base of the cake using a little sugarpaste softened with clear alcohol to hold it in place at the back of the cake. Secure the broad pale yellow satin ribbon to the cake drum's edge using non-toxic glue.

3 Insert the posy pick into the top of the cake and insert the handle of the bouquet into it. Use fine-nose pliers to gently reposition and curve any of the flower and leaf stems that require it.

Hawaiian perfume flower tree

There are about 50 species of *Fagraea* – often known as the perfume flower tree. The tree takes an epiphytic form, not as a parasite, but uses other trees as a support. The trees are native to South East Asia through to northern Australia and the Pacific Islands. The flowers are thick and fleshy in form, opening in the morning and lasting for two days. They fade from a green-tinged white flower through to a cream yellow. The flowers are pollinated by insects and birds, which return later to feed on the red pulp in which the seeds are embedded.

MATERIALS

26-, 24-, 22- and 20-gauge white wires
Wire cutters
Mid-green, pale lemon and white flowerpaste
Edelweiss, vine, sunflower, daffodil, plum, foliage, aubergine and woodland petal dusts
Edible spray varnish
Fresh egg white
Nile green floristry tape

EQUIPMENT

Large rose petal cutters (TT776-778) or see templates on p 140
Non-stick board
Fine tweezers
Fine-nose pliers
Dusting brushes, including a flat dusting brush
Plain-edge cutting wheel
Non-stick rolling pin
Standard set of rose petal cutters (TT276-280)
Foam pad
Large metal ball tool
Wide amaryllis petal veiner (SKGI)
Curved former or kitchen paper
Large datura leaf veiner (Aldaval)

PISTIL

1 Cut a length of 26-gauge white wire in half using wire cutters. Take a small ball of well-kneaded mid-green flowerpaste and insert the wire into it. Work the flowerpaste quickly and firmly down the wire to create a length that measures about two-thirds the length of the petal cutter/template. Leave a small ball/bead of flowerpaste at the tip of the wire and keep the length of the pistil fairly fine. Smooth the length between your palms or against the non-stick board. Use fine tweezers to pinch three very subtle sections to the tip. Curve the length slightly using fine-nose pliers.

2 Dust the tip and length of the pistil with a mixture of edelweiss petal dust mixed with vine. Allow to dry and then spray gently with edible spray varnish.

STAMEN – FILAMENTS

3 Cut three 26-gauge white wires in half and set one piece of wire to one side as you only need to make five stamens for this flower. Attach a ball of well-kneaded white flowerpaste to the wire and work the paste up to the tip of the wire to create a thickened filament. Remove any excess flowerpaste and smooth the length between your palms or against the non-stick board. Repeat to make five stamens. Allow them to rest a little before curving them into a lazy 'S' shape.

ANTHERS

4 Form a ball of pale lemon flowerpaste into a cigar shape. Moisten the tip of the wired filament with fresh egg white and attach the cigar to the end of it. Pinch it firmly in place to secure the two together. Use the plain-edge cutting wheel to mark a single line down the length of the upper surface. Repeat with all five stamens and then leave to dry.

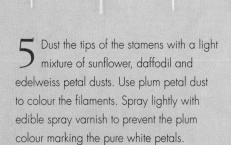

5 Dust the tips of the stamens with a light mixture of sunflower, daffodil and edelweiss petal dusts. Use plum petal dust to colour the filaments. Spray lightly with edible spray varnish to prevent the plum colour marking the pure white petals.

6 Tape the five stamens to the underside of the pistil using half-width nile green floristry tape.

PETALS

7 The petals are fairly fleshy so don't roll the flowerpaste too fine, however, be careful not to make it too heavy either, otherwise the wires will not support the weight of the petals. Roll out some well-kneaded white flowerpaste, leaving a thicker ridge to hold the wire. Cut out the petal shape using one of the three sizes of squashed rose petal cutters or using a plain-edge cutting wheel and the petal template on page 140.

8 Insert a moistened half-length of 24-gauge white wire into the ridge to support about half the length of the petal. As you insert the wire, support the thick ridge on either side of the petal between your finger and thumb and hold the wire very close to the end that is being inserted so that the wire does not pierce through the flowerpaste or bend and change direction while you are carrying out this step.

9 Place the petal onto the foam pad or the palm of your hand and soften the edges using a rolling action with the large end of a metal ball tool. Next, place the petal in between the double-sided wide amaryllis petal veiner and press firmly to texture the surface. Repeat to make five petals. Cover the petals with a plastic bag as you make them to stop them from drying out too much.

10 Take each petal in turn and pinch them from the base very gently through to the tip to create a more natural shape, curving gracefully at the tip. Repeat with each petal and allow them to firm up a little over a curved former or use a few sheets of kitchen paper rolled up. Keep checking on the petals as they are quite large and often lose their shape over the former so you will need to reshape them a little from time to time.

11 Using a flat dusting brush, colour the base of each petal with a mixture of vine and edelweiss petal dusts, fading the colour out as it hits the mid section of the petals.

12 Tape the five petals around the curved stamens and pistil using half-width nile green floristry tape. If the petals are still pliable, then this is good as it will enable you to reshape one last time to create a more realistic effect.

13 The back of the flower fuses the petals together into a tube. To create this, add a ball of white flowerpaste at the base of the petals and work it a little down the stem to create a more slender base. Remove any excess flowerpaste from the base.

CALYX

14 Roll out some mid-green flowerpaste not too thinly and cut out three sepals using the largest of the standard rose petal set squashed a little to create a more narrow sepal shape. Dust the back of the flower with the edelweiss and vine mixture.

15 Soften the edge of each sepal using the metal ball tool and then hollow out the centre of each sepal using the same tool. Moisten the base of each sepal with fresh egg white and attach them with the point at the base around the base of the flower. Pinch and curl the edges a little using your fingers and thumb.

16 Dust the calyx with a mixture of foliage and vine petal dusts. Add tinges of aubergine petal dust to the edges.

BUDS

17 These are rather large. I decided not to use them in the bouquet for this book. However, follow these instructions if you choose to use them. Bend a large hook in the end of a 22-gauge white wire. Form a ball of well-kneaded white flowerpaste into a teardrop shape.

18 Moisten the hooked wire with fresh egg white and insert it into the broad base of the teardrop. Work the base down onto the wire to create a more slender neck shape.

19 Next, pinch five flanges to represent petals using your fingers and fine tweezers. Twist the petals around the bud. Dust as for the back of the flower. The smaller buds would be greener than the larger forms. Add a calyx as for the flower, gauging the size of cutter accordingly.

LEAVES

20 These, like the flowers, are rather large and fairly fleshy. Roll out some mid-green well-kneaded flowerpaste, leaving a thick ridge for the wire. Cut out the leaf either freehand using the plain-edge cutting wheel or use one of the templates on page 140.

21 Insert a 24- or 22-gauge white wire into the thick ridge to support about a third to two-thirds the length of the leaf. Pinch the base of the leaf down onto the wire. Place the leaf onto the foam pad and soften the edges using the large metal ball tool.

22 Texture the leaf using the large double-sided datura leaf veiner. Remove the leaf from the veiner and pinch it from the base through to the tip to accentuate the central vein. Allow to dry fairly flat.

23 Dust in layers with woodland petal dust, fading towards the edges and then over-dust with foliage and a touch of vine. The backs are much paler with more vine colouring. Add aubergine tinges very lightly to the edges. Allow to dry and then glaze lightly with edible spray varnish.

Chinese yam (*Dioscorea*)

This plant belongs to a genus that contains around 600 tropical and subtropical herbaceous climbing plants. There are many decorative forms, some with spotted leaves, others with silver and dark green margins. The backs of the leaves are often decorative too, with plum, magenta or aubergine colouring.

PREPARATION

1 The heart-shaped golden wings rose cutters and the black bryony leaf cutters are ideal for making these decorative yam leaves, however, they will need to be squashed to reshape the design a little to match the templates on page 140.

LEAVES

2 Roll out some mid-green flowerpaste, leaving a thick ridge for the wire. Cut out the leaf shape using one of the various sizes of golden wings rose or black bryony leaf cutters, or refer to the templates on page 140.

3 Insert a 28-, 26- or 24-gauge white wire moistened with fresh egg white into the central thick ridge to support about half the length of the leaf. The exact gauge will depend on the size of the leaf, but remember: the higher the wire gauge number, the finer the wire is.

4 Place the leaf on the foam pad or the palm of your hand and soften the cut edge of the leaf using the medium or large metal ball tool. Use a rolling action with the tool, working half on the flowerpaste and half on your pad/hand.

5 Place the leaf into the double-sided galex or black bryony leaf veiner and press firmly to create a realistic leaf texture. Remove the leaf from the veiner and carefully pinch it from the base through to the tip to accentuate the central vein and add movement to the leaf. Dry over some dimpled foam or crumpled kitchen paper to help support the leaf in a natural shape. Repeat to make the required number of leaves in varying sizes.

6 Dust the leaves in layers on the front surface using a mixture of moss, foliage and vine petal dusts. Dust the back of the leaves with a mixture of plum and aubergine, fading towards the edges. Next, dilute a little plum and aubergine petal dusts with isopropyl alcohol and, using a fine paintbrush, add detail veining from the base of the leaf fading into a fine point on each of the radiating textured veins. Allow to dry. Add a tinge of dry plum/aubergine to the painted area. Spray lightly with edible spray varnish.

7 Tape the leaves onto a length of 22-gauge white wire using half-width nile green floristry tape. Leave a little of each leaf stem showing and stagger them down the stem graduating in size. Add tendrils using curled lengths of pale green 33-gauge wire if desired. I decided to omit the tendrils for the perfume perfection project.

MATERIALS

Mid-green flowerpaste

28-, 26-, 24- and 22-gauge white wires

Fresh egg white

33-gauge pale green wires (optional)

Moss, foliage, vine, plum and aubergine petal dusts

Isopropyl alcohol

Edible spray varnish

Nile green floristry tape

EQUIPMENT

Golden wings rose cutters (TT770-775) or Black bryony leaf cutters (TT652-654) or see templates on p 140

Non-stick rolling pin

Foam pad

Medium or large metal ball tool

Galex leaf veiner (SC) or Black bryony leaf veiner (SKGI)

Dimpled foam or kitchen paper

Dusting brushes

Fine paintbrush

Ylang-ylang

The genus *Cananga* contains two species ranging through tropical Asia into Australia. *Cananga odorata*, a native of Malaysia, is now cultivated in many other tropical areas of the world and is often grown as a commercial crop to create the perfume known as ylang-ylang. The flowers can be yellow or more green in form, and the green-black berries also form a very useful decorative addition to the sugarcrafter's repertoire.

MATERIALS

28-, 26-, 24- and 22-gauge white wires
Pale vine green and mid-green flowerpaste
Vine, moss, sunflower, daffodil, foliage, black, aubergine and edelweiss petal dusts
Fresh egg white
Nile green floristry tape
Edible spray varnish

EQUIPMENT

Piping bag fitted with a no.3 piping tube
Fine paintbrush, dusting brushes
Non-stick rolling pin
Single petal daisy cutter
Scalpel
Foam pad
Medium metal ball tool
Stargazer B petal veiner
Plain-edge cutting wheel
Large gardenia leaf veiner (SKGI)
Fine-nose pliers
Ceramic tool

STAMEN CENTRE

1 Bend a hook in the end of a third length of 28-gauge white wire. Attach a small ball of pale vine green flowerpaste onto the hook. Squeeze the flowerpaste around the wire to secure the two together. Next, use two fingers and thumb to pinch and form the flowerpaste into a triangular shape. Keep the top of the shape flat. Use the no.3 piping tube to emboss a spot at the centre of the shape.

2 Use a mixture of vine and moss petal dusts to dust the embossed spot an intense green. Dust the outer area with sunflower petal dust. Allow to dry.

PETALS

3 Roll out some well-kneaded pale green flowerpaste, leaving a thick ridge for the wire. Angle the rolling pin as you roll the flowerpaste to create a tapered ridge. Cut out the petal shape with the ridge running down the centre using the single petal daisy cutter or a scalpel and the template on page 140.

4 Insert a 28-gauge white wire moistened with fresh egg white into the rounded broader base of the petal to support about a third of the length of the petal. Hold the ridge firmly as you insert the wire to prevent the wire piercing through the flowerpaste. Next, place the petal onto the foam pad or on the palm of your hand and soften the edge using the medium metal ball tool, working half on your pad/hand and half on the edge of the flowerpaste. Take care not to ruffle or frill the edges – you are simply trying to thin and remove the harsh cut edge left by the cutter.

5 Texture the surface of the petal using the double-sided stargazer B petal veiner. Remove the petal from the veiner and carefully pinch the base of the petal through to the tip. Use the metal ball tool to hollow out the base of the petal. Repeat to make six petals. The petals can curve inwards or outwards on one flower – they are quite random in form.

COLOURING AND ASSEMBLY

6 It is best to dust the petals while they are freshly made and still pliable so that the colour sticks well and you can reshape the petals during assembly. Dust the petals as desired: they can be green in form, green-yellow or a golden yellow. Here I have used a mixture of daffodil, sunflower and edelweiss white petal dusts.

7 Tape three inner petals evenly spaced around the stamen centre using quarter-width nile green floristry tape. Pinch and curl the tips of each petal to create more movement. Next, tape the remaining three petals to fill the gaps in the first layer. Once again, pinch the tips and curl them inwards or outwards as desired. Dust the base and the tips of each petal with a mixture of moss and vine petal dusts. Allow to dry and hold them over a jet of steam from a just-boiled kettle or use a clothes steamer to set the colour and take away the dusty effect left by the dusting process.

CALYX

8 There are three tiny sepals at the base of the flower. Form three cone-shaped pieces of pale-green flowerpaste and flatten using the flat side of a veiner. Soften the edges and then pinch at the tip. Attach to the base of the flower using fresh egg white.

LEAVES

9 Roll out some well-kneaded mid-green flowerpaste, leaving a central thick ridge for the wire. Use the plain-edge cutting wheel to cut out a pointed oval-shaped leaf.

10 Insert a 28-, 26- or 24-gauge white wire, depending on the leaf size, moistened with fresh egg white. Soften the edge of the leaf and then texture using the large gardenia leaf veiner. Remove the leaf from the veiner and pinch it from the base to the tip quite firmly to accentuate the central vein. Curve the leaf slightly. Repeat to make numerous leaves in graduating sizes.

11 Dust the leaves in layers, starting with foliage and moss mixed together to add depth at the base and centre of each leaf and fading towards the edges. Over-dust with vine petal dust. Leave to dry and then glaze lightly with edible spray varnish or dip into a half glaze (see page 13).

BERRIES

12 Bend a hook in the end of a 28-gauge white wire using fine-nose pliers. Roll a ball of mid-green flowerpaste and insert the hooked end into it. Work the base of the ball down onto the wire to create a more tear-dropped shaped fruit.

13 Use the rounded end of the ceramic tool to create indents and bumps over the surface of the fruit. Repeat to make berries in varying sizes. Tape over each wire with quarter-width nile green floristry tape.

14 Dust the fruit to the desired stage of ripeness using layers of vine and foliage, gradually introducing black and aubergine petal dusts, and then just black. It is wise to dust these quickly so that the colour is intense and sticks easily to the flowerpaste.

Allow to dry, then spray the berries to create a glossy finish using edible spray glaze or dip into a full glaze (see page 13).

15 Using quarter-width nile green floristry tape, tape the berries into clusters of varying numbers, leaving a little of each stem showing.

Perfumed perfection bouquet

A fairly traditional bouquet shape using very unconventional flowers and foliage. That is the beauty of making flowers in sugar or cold porcelain – artistic licence allows the creator to use whatever components they fancy.

MATERIALS AND EQUIPMENT

22- and 20-gauge white wires

Nile green floristry tape

Fine-nose pliers

Wire cutters or floristry scissors

FLOWERS AND FOLIAGE

5 trailing stems of decorative yam foliage (p 21)

3 white perfume flowers (p 18)

7 ylang-ylang flowers (p 22)

15 ylang-ylang leaves (p 23)

5 groups of ylang-ylang berries (p 23)

5 perfume flower leaves (p 20)

PREPARATION

1 Strengthen any of the flower and foliage stems that require extra support or length by taping 22- or 20-gauge white wires into the main stems using half-width nile green floristry tape. The gauge of the wire will depend on the weight of each item.

ASSEMBLY/CONSTRUCTION

2 Take two lengths of decorative yam foliage, one longer than the other, and bend the end of their stems to a 90-degree angle using fine-nose pliers. Tape the two stems together using half-width nile green floristry tape.

3 Next, add and tape in the three white perfume flowers to create the focal area of the bouquet. Use wire cutters or floristry scissors to trim off any excess bulk created by the wires. Add a third shorter stem of decorative yam foliage to the left-hand side of the bouquet to balance and create the width of the display.

4 Use the ylang-ylang flowers and leaves to fill in the gaps in the bouquet, using a couple of flowers to exend colour to the bottom length of the bouquet.

5 Use the five groups of ylang-ylang berries to add more interest, positioning the smaller groups at the edges of the display.

6 Finally, add the large perfume flower leaves around the focal area to fill in the remaining gaps.

Flamingo floral

This pretty cake features a floral combination of flamingo pink frangipani flowers, flamingo anthuriums and foliage. A simple painted blossom side design completes this cake that would be ideal for a birthday, small wedding or anniversary.

MATERIALS

23 cm (9 in) round fruitcake placed on a thin cake board of the same size

1 kg (2 lb 3 oz) white almond paste

1.5 kg (3 lb 5 oz) pale pink sugarpaste

Fine and broad pink satin ribbons

Clear alcohol (Cointreau or kirsch)

Non-toxic glue stick

Plum, white, coral, aubergine, vine, and foliage petal dusts

Nile green floristry tape

EQUIPMENT

30 cm (12 in) round cake drum

Straight-edged sugarpaste smoother

Fine paintbrush

Wire cutters

Food-grade plastic posy pick

Fine-nose pliers

FLOWERS

5 pink frangipani flowers and 5 leaves (p 54)

3 flamingo anthuriums (p 29)

2 painter's palette anthuriums (p 28)

2 trails of piper foliage (p 136)

2 ladder fern fronds (p 55)

PREPARATION

1 Coat the cake and cake drum as described on pages 11–12. Transfer the cake on top of the cake drum and use the straight-edged sugarpaste smoother to blend the join between the cake and the board. Leave to dry overnight.

2 Attach a band of fine pink satin ribbon around the base of the cake, using a small amount of sugarpaste softened with clear alcohol to hold it in place. Secure the broad pink satin ribbon to the cake drum's edge using non-toxic glue.

SIDE DESIGN

3 Dilute some plum, white and a touch of coral petal dusts with clear alcohol and paint groups of very simple five-petal blossoms onto the surface of the cake and the drum. Increase the depth of colour, adding more plum, coral and a touch of aubergine and then add a dot in the centre of each blossom. Next, dilute a mixture of vine, foliage and white to paint a few leaves into the design.

4 Insert the posy pick into the top of the cake and place the handle of the spray, as described on page 30, into it. Use fine-nose pliers to rearrange and position any of the floral elements to create a more pleasing design.

Anthurium

These exotic heart-shaped flowers originate from the rain forests of Columbia, although they are now cultivated in most flower-growing areas of the world. They are often known as 'painter's palette' flowers and exist in a vast selection of colour combinations.

MATERIALS

Fresh anthuruim flower

White flowerpaste

24- and 22-gauge white wires

Fresh egg white

Cornflower

Sunflower, daffodil, edelweiss, plum, coral, vine, moss-green aubergine and ruby petal dusts

Edible spray varnish

Nile green floristry tape

EQUIPMENT

Homemade spadix veiner (see opposite)

Non-stick rolling pin

Dusting brushes

Plain-edge cutting wheel

Foam pad

Large metal ball tool

Flamingo anthurium spathe veiner (Aldaval)

Dimple foam

Cotton wool

Fine paintbrush

SPADIX

1 First of all you need to buy a fresh anthurium flower to make a mould of the pointed textured spadix. Try to find a flower that has plenty of raised dots on the surface of the spadix. Use a silicone moulding paste (see page 7 for more information on making a mould). Form a ball of well-kneaded white flowerpaste and insert a 22-gauge white wire moistened with fresh egg white into it. Work the paste down the wire to create the required length and thickness – this does vary quite a bit between the various types of anthurium. Place the spadix into the silicone mould. Squeeze the sides of the mould against the soft flowerpaste to texture the surface, then remove from the mould. Allow to set a little and decide if you want a straight spadix or a slightly curved one. This will depend on the variety you are making. Allow to dry.

SPATHE

2 Roll out some white flowerpaste (or your chosen colour) fairly thickly leaving a thicker ridge for the wire. Remember this is quite a waxy flower and the veiner has strong veins that will cut through the paste if it is too thin. Insert a 22-gauge white wire moistened with fresh egg white into the thick ridge to support about half the length. Dust the flowerpaste with cornflour and carefully position it into the double-sided anthurium spathe veiner. Press the two sides of the veiner firmly into the paste to texture it.

3 Remove the shape from the mould and carefully cut out around the edge with the plain-edge cutting wheel or a pair of sharp scissors. Pinch the paste down the centre and then dry on some dimpled foam with pads of cotton wool or kitchen paper to support the shape.

COLOURING

4 The colouring will depend on the variety you are making. The spadix shown has been dusted at the base with a mixture of coral and plum petal dusts and a mix of vine and moss green at the tip. Colour the spathe as desired. Here, vine green and edelweiss petal dusts have been used with an over dust of vine and moss green to catch the edges and ridges of the spathe. The darker forms have been coloured to various degrees with coral and plum and an overdusting of aubergine. Spray with edible spray varnish to give a glossy finish. Tape the spadix onto the spathe with half-width nile green floristry tape.

Flamingo flower

Anthurium scherzeranum is native to Guatemala and Costa Rica. They have a gentle shape and veining, and once again, the colour range is vast. Its common name comes from the curly formation of the spadix.

SPADIX

1 Attach a ball of well-kneaded white flowerpaste to the end of a 24-gauge white wire. Work the flowerpaste down the wire to create a slender spadix. Texture it using either a nutmeg grater or a homemade spadix veiner. Allow to firm up a little before curling into a flamingo neck shape.

2 Dust as desired. The paler pink flower pictured has the spadix dusted with a light mixture of sunflower, daffodil and edelweiss petal dusts. The two darker flowers were dusted at the base fading towards the tip with a mixture of plum, coral and edelweiss petal dusts. Use a little of the colour from the tip towards the base too, leaving a paler area mid-way.

SPATHE

3 Roll out some well-kneaded white or pale-coloured flowerpaste, leaving a thick ridge for the wire. Use the template on page 141 and the plain-edge cutting wheel to cut out the spathe, or simply cut out freehand. Insert a 24- or 22-gauge white wire moistened with fresh egg white into the thick ridge to support about a third to half the length.

4 Place the wired spathe onto the foam pad and soften the edges, working half on the flowerpaste and half on the foam pad with a large metal ball tool. Use a rolling action to thin the edge, but do not frill. Texture the spathe using the double-sided flamingo anthurium spathe veiner. Press firmly to give a stronger veining. Remove and hollow out the back slightly using your fingers and thumb. Curve the shape as desired. Pinch from the base through to the tip to accentuate the central vein. Leave to dry, supported with dimpled foam and cotton wool.

COLOURING

5 The flowers pictured were dusted using a mixture of plum, coral and edelweiss petal dusts. Working from the base fading out towards the middle, catch the edges and increase the colour at the tip. Introduce a light mixture of vine and edelweiss, or use aubergine petal dust to create a very dark spathe colour. The darkest of the three flowers has extra depth of colour, added by painting the spathe with a mixture of isopropyl alcohol and aubergine, and also veins added using a diluted mixture of ruby petal dust and isopropyl alcohol. Tape the spadix onto the spathe using half-width nile green floristry tape. Allow to dry and then spray a few times lightly with edible spray varnish.

MATERIALS

White flowerpaste

24- and 22-gauge white wires

Sunflower, daffodil, edelweiss, plum, coral, vine, aubergine and ruby petal dusts

Fresh egg white

Isopropyl alcohol

Nile green floristry tape

Edible spray varnish

EQUIPMENT

Nutmeg grater or homemade spadix veiner (see opposite)

Dusting brushes

Non-stick rolling pin

Plain-edge cutting wheel

Foam pad

Large metal ball tool

Flamingo anthurium spathe veiner (Aldaval)

Dimple foam

Cotton wool

Fine paintbrush

Frangipani bouquet

Flamingo anthuriums and bright pink frangipani flowers are a perfect combination in this exotic spray of flowers. Trailing stems of pink-veined piper foliage and fern leaves help to soften the edges of the design.

MATERIALS

22-gauge white wires

Nile green floristry tape

Wire cutters

Fine-nose pliers

FLOWERS

5 pink frangipani flowers, plus foliage (p 54)

2 painter's palette anthuriums (p 28)

3 assorted flamingo anthuriums (p 29)

3 ladder fern leaves (p 55)

3 trails of piper foliage (p 136)

PREPARATION

1 Tape 22-gauge white wires onto any of the flower and foliage stems that require extra length or support using half-width nile green floristry tape.

COLOURING

2 Start the spray by simply gathering the five frangipani flowers together into a posy shape using half-width nile green floristry tape.

3 Next, surround the frangipani flowers with the painter's palette anthuriums and the flamingo anthuriums. Trim off any excess bulk wire as you work using wire cutters.

4 Fill in the gaps around the flowers using the frangipani leaves and the ladder fern fronds. Use fine-nose pliers to reposition any of the elements as you work.

5 To complete the spray, add the trails of piper foliage, which will lengthen the spray and soften the edges too.

3

4

Butterflies and flowers

Stencilled butterflies echo and complement the more dominant butterfly flowers of the trailing bouquet on this small birthday cake design.

MATERIALS

15 cm (6 in) curved heart-shaped fruitcake placed on a thin cake board of the same size

23 cm (9 in) round cake drum

450 g (1 lb) white almond paste

450g (1 lb) white sugarpaste

Fine and broad orange satin ribbon

Clear alcohol (Cointreau or kirsch)

Non-toxic glue stick

Small amount of white flowerpaste

Vine, white, tangerine, coral and aubergine petal dusts

EQUIPMENT

Straight-edged sugarpaste smoother

Non-stick rolling pin

Non-stick board

Butterfly stencil (J)

Dusting brushes

Scalpel

Fine paintbrush

Non-slip mat

Perspex tilting cake stand (Cc)

FLOWERS

Butterfly flower bouquet (p 40)

PREPARATION

1 Cover the cake and cake drum as described on pages 11–12. Position the cake on top of the coated drum and use the straight-edge sugarpaste smoother to blend the join between the cake and board. Allow to dry for a few days.

2 Attach a band of fine orange satin ribbon to the base of the cake, using a small amount of sugarpaste softened with clear alcohol to hold it in place. Secure a band of broad orange satin ribbon to the cake drum's edge using non-toxic glue.

STENCIL DESIGN

3 Roll out a little well-kneaded white flowerpaste thinly onto the non-stick board. Peel the flowerpaste off the board and flip it over so that the sticky side is uppermost. Place the butterfly stencil on top of the sticky flowerpaste to hold it in place. Next, use petal dusts to colour in the various sections of the butterfly design. Use a mixture of vine and white petal dusts at the base of each wing. Use tangerine and coral petal dusts mixed together for the outer area of each wing.

4 Remove the stencil from flowerpaste. Use the scalpel to cut out around the dusted butterfly design. Place to one side and repeat the process to create three stencilled butterflies. Attach onto the cake and drum using clear alcohol. Dilute some aubergine petal dust with clear alcohol and paint the body and antennae using a fine paintbrush and then add spots to the wings and detail to the tips of each wing section too.

5 Assemble the butterfly bouquet as described on page 40. Put a piece of non-slip mat onto the tilt of the Perspex cake stand and place the cake on top of it. Rest and position the butterfly bouquet at the base of the cake stand to complete the design.

Butterfly flower tree

The flowers of this beautiful tree from Central to Southern America are between 15–20 cm (6–8 in) across. Here, I have scaled the flower down for use on cakes. The flowers can be yellow, apricot, through to a deep orange in colour. The scent of the flower is almost like that of an apricot. They are fairly simple to make, only having five petals, and yet form a stunning focal flower for cake design.

PISTIL

1 The pistil is split into three very fine sections. Cut three short lengths of 33-gauge white wire. Take a tiny ball of pale tangerine flowerpaste and work it onto one length of wire, about 2.5 cm (1 in) from the tip. Hold the wire firmly between one finger and thumb and use the other finger and thumb to twiddle the paste towards the end. Keep thinning the paste and remove any excess as you work to create a very finely coated wire. Repeat with the other two wires and gently curve them.

2 Tape the three sections together using quarter-width nile green floristry tape. Next, attach a ball of pale green flowerpaste at the base of the pistil. Work the base into a slightly oval shape and divide into three sections using the plain-edge cutting wheel. Set to one side.

STAMENS

3 To make the filaments (lengths of the stamens), cut five short lengths of 33-gauge white wire. Attach a slightly larger ball of pale green flowerpaste than that used for the pistil onto a wire. Work the flowerpaste as for the pistil, creating a tapered shape slightly broader at the base and fine at the tip. Smooth the length between your palms or against the non-stick board. Next, flatten the shape using the flat side of the stargazer B petal veiner. If the shape is too heavy or has very uneven edges, simply trim them into shape using a pair of fine scissors.

MATERIALS

33-, 28-, 26-, 24- and 22-gauge white wires
Pale tangerine, pale green, pale yellow and mid-green flowerpaste
Nile green floristry tape
Coral, tangerine, vine, daffodil, sunflower, white, foliage and aubergine petal dusts
Fresh egg white
Edible spray varnish

EQUIPMENT

Wire cutters
Plain-edge cutting wheel
Non-stick board
Stargazer B petal veiner
Fine scissors
Dusting brushes
Non-stick rolling pin

Amaryllis petal cutter (TT) or see template on p 140
Foam pad
Large metal ball tool
Ceramic silk veining tool
Fine scissors
Sage leaf or cattleya orchid wing petal cutter
Mandevilla leaf veiner (SKGI)

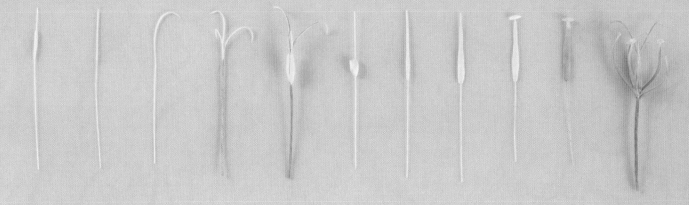

4 To create the anther, take a tiny piece of pale yellow flowerpaste and form it into a cigar shape. Moisten the tip of the filament with water and embed it into the centre of the anther to secure the two together. Mark a line down the length of the anther using the plain-edge cutting wheel. Repeat to complete the five stamens. Curve the length of each stamen before they have a chance to dry.

COLOURING AND ASSEMBLY

5 Dust each fine section of the pistil and the length of each stamen filament with a mixture of coral and tangerine petal dusts. Dust the green ovary with vine petal dust. Use a mixture of daffodil and sunflower petal dusts to colour the anthers.

6 Tape the five stamens around the ovary/pistil using quarter-width nile green floristry tape so that they curve in towards the pistil. Set to one side.

PETALS

7 Take a piece of well-kneaded pale tangerine flowerpaste and roll it out using the non-stick rolling pin to leave a thick ridge for the wire. As you roll the flowerpaste, try to angle it so that it creates a tapered ridge. Cut out the petal shape using the amaryllis petal cutter or use the template on page 140 and the plain-edge cutting wheel. Insert a 26-gauge white wire moistened with fresh egg white into the thick ridge to support about a third of the length of the petal – hold the wire very close to the end that is being inserted so that it can't wiggle and pierce through the flowerpaste.

8 Place the petal onto your palm or a firm foam pad and soften the edge using the large metal ball tool, working half on the edge of the petal and half on your palm/foam pad. Next, place the petal into the double-sided stargazer B petal veiner and press firmly to texture the surface.

9 Remove the petal from the veiner and place it back onto the foam pad. Use the plain-edge cutting wheel to draw three fine lines down the centre of the petal. Pick up the petal and pinch it gently from behind at the base working through to the tip to accentuate the central veins and give the petal more shape and movement. The tip should be pinched slightly harder.

10 The edges can be fairly flat or slightly frilled. I prefer the frilled effect as it gives the flower more movement. Rest the petal against your index finger and use the ceramic silk veining tool to frill the upper edges of the petal. Take care not to point the tip of the tool into the flowerpaste as this will create ugly indents. Finally, curve the petal and dry over a dimpled foam pad or curved former. Repeat to make five petals for each flower.

COLOURING AND ASSEMBLY

11 Dust each petal to the required colour/depth. Here I have used a mixture of coral and tangerine petal dusts. Add white petal dust for a paler colour. Start by adding a streak of colour from the base of each petal fading out towards the edges on the back and front. Bring some of the colour in from the edge of each petal, catching the side of the brush against the edges to make it more intense on the very edge.

12 Tape the petals evenly spaced around the base of the stamens using half-width nile green floristry tape. If the petals are still pliable reshape them as required.

CALYX

13 There are five sepals to the calyx. I find it best to wire each section giving the whole flower a lot more movement. Cut five short lengths of 28-gauge white wire. Work a small ball of well-kneaded pale yellow flowerpaste onto the wire to create a tapered shape measuring just under 3.5 cm (1.5 in) long. Work the paste onto the wire in the same way that the stamen filaments were made. Smooth the length of the shape between your palms and then place onto the non-stick board and flatten it with the flat side of the stargazer B petal veiner. Trim the shape with a pair of fine scissors if needed.

14 Place the sepal into the stargazer B veiner and press firmly to texture it. Remove the sepal from the veiner and pinch it from the base through to the tip to create a central vein and a sharper point. Repeat to make five sepals. Dust each sepal with a mixture of sunflower and a touch of daffodil petal dusts, starting at the base and fading out towards the tip. Add a tinge of vine to the very tips to break up the space.

15 Tape the five sepals onto the back of the flower using half-width nile green floristry tape. Position them in the spaces in between each petal.

LEAVES

16 Cut lengths of 26-, 24- or 22-gauge white wire into half lengths. Roll out well-kneaded mid-green flowerpaste, leaving a thick ridge for the wire. Use a sage leaf or cattleya orchid wing petal cutter to cut out the shape.

17 Insert a 24-gauge white wire into the thick ridge of the leaf to support half the length of the leaf. Place leaf on foam pad and soften edges using the large metal ball tool. Place the leaf in mandevilla leaf veiner, lining the tip of the leaf and the base with the central vein. Remove and pinch from base to tip to accentuate the central vein. Allow to dry slightly.

COLOURING AND GLAZING

18 Dust the leaf in layers, starting with foliage petal dust from the base of the leaf, aiming the colour down the central vein first of all and then fading towards the edges. Over-dust with vine petal dust. Add a tinge of aubergine here and there to break up the space. Allow to dry and then spray very lightly with edible spray varnish.

Zantedeschia berries

The red, green and gold berries of the African *zantedeschia* family can be a wonderful addition to exotic flower arrangements. The plant is often called calla lily, although strictly speaking it does not belong to the lily family.

BERRIES

1 Cut several lengths of 30-gauge white wire into fifths using wire cutters or sharp florist's scissors. Use fine-nose pliers to bend a hook in the end of each wire. Use a lighter or tea-light flame to singe the white paper off the wires to give a black finish.

2 Roll the pale green, pale yellow and orange-red flowerpaste into lots of small berries. Moisten the hooked end of a singed wire with fresh egg white and thread it through the centre of a berry, leaving a little of the wire showing through.

3 Create a series of indents radiating from the hook into the berry. Repeat to create numerous berries – the number varies quite a bit, which is good for flower arranging as more variation can be created.

4 Tape over a 22-gauge white wire with white floristry tape and then start to tape the berries to the wire in no particular colour order – although I usually fix the green berries at the top of the stem.

5 It is easier to dust the berries once they are all taped onto the stem. Dust vine, moss, sunflower, tangerine, red and ruby petal dusts over the berries, creating a natural ripening process from green through to a rich red. The odd tinge of aubergine to the rich red berries can help to add extra depth. Allow to dry and then dip into a full confectioner's glaze or spray a few times with edible spray varnish, allowing the glaze to set in between coats.

6 Next, thicken the stem with a strip of shredded kitchen paper. Tape over the top with half-width nile green floristry tape. Use the side of a pair of scissors to rub the blade against the tape to smooth out the joins in the tape and leave a slightly polished finish.

BRACT

7 This is the left-over dead flower often removed by florists so you might feel that you don't want to add it. I use a short length of white floristry tape dusted with cream and nutkin brown petal dusts. Use the fine end of the dresden tool to draw a series of fine lines onto the tape. Cut into the edge with a scalpel or sharp pair of scissors to give a ragged finish. Tape the bract onto the base of the berries using half-width nile green floristry tape. Polish the stem and then dust lightly with vine and foliage petal dusts. Spray the stem lightly with edible spray varnish.

MATERIALS

30- and 22-gauge white wires

Pale green, pale yellow and orange-red flowerpaste

Fresh egg white

White and nile green floristry tape

Vine, moss, sunflower, tangerine, red, ruby, aubergine, cream, nutkin brown and foliage petal dusts

Full confectioner's glaze (see p 13) or edible spray varnish

Kitchen paper

EQUIPMENT

Wire cutters or sharp florist's scissors

Fine-nose pliers

Lighter or tea light

Dusting brushes

Scissors

Dresden tool

Scalpel or sharp scissors

Joseph's coat foliage

There are about 16 species of *Codiaeum* that are found native from Malaysia to the Pacific, as well as many cultivated forms that are grown in other areas of the world too. In the UK, the plants are often cultivated as houseplants and known as *Croton*, or affectionately as Joseph's coat because of the interesting colour range of their leathery ornate foliage. They are very useful leaves, filling lots of space and providing extra colour to floral displays. The size and shape of each variety is different, as are the colour variations. Here I have illustrated some of my favourites.

MATERIALS

Pale green or cream flowerpaste

24-, 22- or 20-gauge white wires

Cornflour

Sunflower, daffodil, coral, plum, foliage, vine, woodland, ruby and forest petal dusts

Isopropyl alcohol

Edible spray varnish

EQUIPMENT

Non-stick rolling pin

Grooved board

Scalpel

Plain-edge cutting wheel

Foam pad

Large metal ball tool

Large, flat dusting brushes

Large gardenia or mandevilla leaf veiner (SKGI)

Dimpled foam

Cotton wool or kitchen paper

Fine paintbrush

Toothbrush or stencil brush

Rubber gloves (optional)

LEAVES

1 These leaves are quite fleshy so there is no need to roll the flowerpaste super fine. Take some well-kneaded pale green or cream flowerpaste and roll it out, leaving a thicker ridged area for the wire. A grooved board may be used for this if desired.

2 Cut out the Croton leaf shape using one of the templates on page 141 and a scalpel or plain-edge cutting wheel.

3 Insert a white wire, the size of which is dependent on the size of the leaf, moistened with fresh egg white into the thick ridge of the leaf to support at least half the length. For the finer tri-lobed shapes it is important to support as much of the leaf length as possible.

4 Place the leaf against the foam pad and soften the edges of the leaf with the large metal ball tool, working half on the very edge of the leaf and half on the foam pad using a rolling action with the tool rather than rubbing it, which would create a frilled edge.

5 Next, dust the leaf with cornflour to prevent sticking and place it into the large gardenia or mandevilla leaf veiner. Line up the tip of the leaf and the base with the central vein of the leaf veiner. Press firmly to texture the surface of the leaf.

6 Remove the leaf from the veiner and carefully pinch it from the base through to the tip to shape it and emphasize the central vein. If you are making a tri-lobed leaf, you will need to pinch the leaf down to the tip too.

7 The thick flowerpaste at the very base of the leaf now needs to be worked between your finger and thumb to create a fleshy stem. Alternatively, extra flowerpaste can be added to the stem when the leaf has dried and blended between your finger and thumb. Allow the leaf to dry slightly before colouring. Rest it on some dimpled foam. Use cotton wool or kitchen paper under the side sections of a tri-lobed leaf to give it support and more movement.

COLOURING

8 The leaves illustrated here have various colour combinations. The first leaf pictured is dusted gently with a mixture of sunflower and daffodil petal dusts and then over-dusted from the base with a mixture of coral and plum petal dusts. The edges of the leaf are dusted with foliage and vine petal dusts. Painted veins are added using isopropyl alcohol mixed with foliage petal dust and a touch of woodland. Use a fine paintbrush to paint in the stronger central vein and then add finer side veins. Allow to dry, then spray with edible spray varnish – this works better if built up in layers, otherwise the leaves become too shiny.

9 The smaller red leaf pictured was dusted with a mixture of ruby and plum petal dusts. Darker green shading was dusted onto the base and the tip using woodland petal dust. Spots and a central vein were painted on using woodland diluted with isopropyl alcohol. Other variations use ruby petal dust diluted with isopropyl alcohol.

10 The fine spotted effect on the larger three leaves can be created using a mixture of foliage with a touch of forest or woodland diluted with isopropyl alcohol and then flicked over the leaves using a toothbrush kept only for this purpose or a stencil brush – something with stiff bristles is required here. A pair of food-safety rubber gloves could be good here too to avoid green fingers. Stains can be removed, however, using diluted bicarbonate of soda.

Butterfly flower bouquet

Exotic orange butterfly flowers have huge impact in this eye-catching bouquet combined with Joseph's coat foliage and *Zantedeschia* berries. The display is completed with the addition of a tropical fantasy butterfly.

MATERIALS AND EQUIPMENT

22-gauge white wires

Nile green floristry tape

Green, yellow and orange paper-covered decorative wires

Wire cutters

Yew wood vase (optional)

FLOWERS

3 orange butterfly flowers and 5 leaves (p 34–36)

7 Joseph's coat leaves (p 38)

3 stems of *Zantedeschia* berries (p 37)

1 fantasy butterfly (p 92)

PREPARATION

1 Strengthen the flower or foliage stems by taping 22-gauge white wire onto the main stems using half-width nile green floristry tape. Take a few lengths of green, yellow and orange paper-covered decorative wires and plait them together – not too neatly or tightly.

ASSEMBLY

2 Tape together the three orange butterfly flowers into a group using the largest/prettiest flower as the focal point. Add a few of its own foliage to fill in the gaps.

3 Use the Joseph's coat leaves to surround and frame the flowers. Trim off any excess bulk wire from the handle at the back of the bouquet using wire cutters. Tape over with half-width nile green floristry tape.

4 Use the *zantedeschia* berries spaced around the flowers to extend the shape of the bouquet and add further interest.

5 Finally, add the length of plaited paper-covered decorative wires to trail at the base of the bouquet. Use a few more loops of wire at the back of the bouquet too. Tape over the handle of the bouquet with full-width nile green floristry tape. Thread the wire of the butterfly into the bouquet and tape it onto the handle. Curve its wire to blend with the plaited wires. Display in a suitable container.

3

4

Moon and sun

The blue moon-like qualities of the beak of this flower and the stark contrast of the sunray-like petals form a striking combination on this unusual and stunning celebration cake that would be suitable as a birthday cake or perhaps a sapphire wedding anniversary cake!

MATERIALS

20 cm (8 in) round rich fruitcake placed on a thin cake board of the same size

750 g (1 lb 10 oz) white almond paste

750 g (1 lb 10 oz) white sugarpaste

Light gold satin ribbon

Clear alcohol (Cointreau or kirsch)

Small amount of white flowerpaste

White bridal satin dust

Vine and foliage petal dusts

Silver cake stand

Food-grade plastic posy pick

EQUIPMENT

Non-stick rolling pin

Non-stick board

Tiny monstera leaf cutter (Ai-mizuke)

Foam pad

Small metal ball tool

Plain-edge cutting wheel

Small dusting brush

Fine paintbrush

Fine-nose pliers

FLOWERS

Moon and sun bouquet (p 50)

PREPARATION

1 Cover the cake as described on pages 11–12. Leave to dry overnight. Attach a band of light gold satin ribbon around the base of the cake using a small amount of sugarpaste softened with clear alcohol to hold it in place.

SIDE DESIGN

2 Roll out some well-kneaded white flowerpaste thinly onto the non-stick board. Use the tiny monstera leaf cutter to cut out several leaf shapes. Place the leaves onto the foam pad and soften the edges using the small metal ball tool.

3 Use the small end of the plain-edge cutting wheel to mark a central vein down each leaf and then add a single side vein to each of the leaf sections. Pick up each leaf and pinch it from the base through to the tip to accentuate the central vein.

4 Attach the leaves to the side and the top surface of the cake using clear alcohol to secure them in place. Leave to dry and then set in place.

5 Next, mix together some white bridal satin dust with a touch of vine petal dust. Use a small dusting brush to gently colour the cut-out leaves, taking care not to get the colour onto the surrounding areas of the cake. Add some detail veining using a fine paintbrush and a mixture of vine and foliage petal dusts diluted with clear alcohol.

ASSEMBLY

6 Place the cake onto the silver cake stand. Assemble the sprays as described on page 50. Insert a food-grade posy pick into the upper surface of the cake. Insert the handle of the larger spray into the posy pick. Use fine-nose pliers to rearrange the various elements of the spray to create a more balanced display on the cake. Create a second smaller spray using remaining flowers and foliage. Place the smaller spray at the base of the silver cake stand to complete the design.

Crane flower

There are five species of *strelitzia* and all are native to South Africa where they are often known as crane flowers or birds of paradise. In fact, they are pollinated by sun birds and bats too. Most folk think of the orange-petalled flowers although they can be yellow, white and creamy-green. The blue arrow-like petals are actually stamens. The white-petalled forms of *strelitzia* are much larger than the more common orange forms and the beak colouring varies too, often being quite strikingly black in colour. I was shocked when I first saw this plant on a brief trip to South Africa – it was about the height of two-storey house!

MATERIALS

White and mid-green flowerpaste
26-, 24-, 20- and 18-gauge white wires
Fresh egg white
Ultramarine and Prussian blue craft dusts
White, vine, daffodil, edelweiss, plum, aubergine, foliage, woodland and forest petal dusts
Edible spray varnish

White and nile green floristry tape
Isopropyl alcohol

EQUIPMENT

Non-stick rolling pin
Plain-edge cutting wheel
Scalpel
Strelitzia cutters (AD)

Dresden tool
Foam pad
Medium and large metal ball tools
Large dusting brushes
Very large tulip leaf veiner (SKGI) or a piece of dried sweetcorn husk
Sharp scissors
Fine angled tweezers

STAMENS

1 Although these dramatic blue structures look like petals they are actually the stamens! As with most blue and purple flowers it is best to use white flowerpaste and then dust to create a clean colour to the finished piece – using a blue flowerpaste tends to create a rather grey finish. Roll out some well-kneaded white flowerpaste, leaving a thick ridge that will run down the length of the stamen. Angle the non-stick rolling pin on either side of the ridge to create a tapered ridge. Use the stamen template on page 141 and the plain-edge cutting wheel or scalpel to cut out the shape or use the stamen cutter from the *strelitzia* cutter set.

2 Insert a 26-gauge white wire moistened with fresh egg white into the thick ridge of the stamen so that it supports most of the length. Next, thin down the narrow part of the

stamen by working the flowerpaste firmly between your finger and thumb. Leave some of the excess bulk that will be gathered at the base and trim off any excess so the length is about that of the original template or cutter shape. Use the broad end of the dresden tool to thin the edges of this section, leaving a slight texture at the same time and a slightly serrated finish to the edges.

3 Place the shape onto the foam pad or the palm of your hand with the ridged side uppermost and soften the edges using the medium metal ball tool. Use the tool to hollow out either side of the arrowhead shape. Pinch the length of the stamen from the base to the tip to create a strong central vein to the front surface of the stamen and to create a sharper point to the shape.

4 Roll out some more white flowerpaste and cut out the small stamen bract shape using the template on page 141 or the appropriate cutter from the *strelitzia* cutter set. Soften the edges using the metal ball tool and then pinch slightly at the tip and the base to create a gentle central vein. Moisten the base of the stamen with fresh egg white and attach the bract onto it. Repeat to make the required number of stamens – there is one stamen to

every three petals and the number does vary depending on the stage of the flower's life. I generally use two or three stamens per flower.

COLOURING

5 Dust the stamens with ultramarine and Prussian blue craft dusts, leaving the very tip and the very base a little paler. Dust the tip of the stamen heavily with white petal dust to represent the pollen. Spray lightly with edible spray varnish.

LARGE PETAL

6 You will need to make two large petals and one smaller petal to add to each stamen. Roll out some well-kneaded white flowerpaste, leaving a central ridge for the wire. Cut out a petal shape using the large petal template on page 141 and the plain-edge cutting wheel or the larger petal cutter from the *strelitzia* cutter set.

7 Insert a 24-gauge white wire moistened with fresh egg white into the thick ridge of the petal to support about half its length. Thin the base of the petal down onto the wire slightly and then trim off any excess flowerpaste. Place the petal onto the foam

pad and soften the edges using the large metal ball tool. Next, place the petal into the very large tulip leaf veiner or sweetcorn husk to texture both sides of the petal.

8 Pinch the petal from the base through to the tip to accentuate the central vein and create a sharper point to the petal too. Repeat to make another large petal.

SMALL PETAL

9 This is made in exactly the same way as the larger petals but you will only need to make one of them and the tip needs to be pinched into a finer, sharper point.

COLOURING AND ASSEMBLY

10 It is best to dust and assemble the petals while still pliable so they can be reshaped to create a more realistic form. Mix together some daffodil, edelweiss and vine petal dusts. Dust each of the petals from the base to the tip, fading the colour towards the tip on both sides of each petal. Use plum petal dust to add an intense colouring at the base of each petal, fading it out as it enters the main petal area. Tinge the very tips of the petals gently with aubergine petal dust.

11 Use half-width white floristry tape to tape the two larger petals together. Next, add a blue stamen followed by a smaller petal. This creates one flowerhead group. You will need two or three groups to make one flower. Tape the groups together onto the end of a few 18-gauge white wires using full-width nile green floristry tape.

12 To form the start of the 'beak' structure, tape over a few 18-gauge white wires with nile green floristry tape and add to the main stem at an angle, taping the two together with full-width nile green floristry tape. Use white flowerpaste to build up the remainder of the beak, blending the flowerpaste against the wire. Smooth the flowerpaste to form a fine point at the tip and work it at the base down onto the main stem to create a neck shape. Allow to dry. The remainder of the stem may be thickened with flowerpaste or with lengths of shredded kitchen paper taped onto the stem with full-width nile green floristry tape.

LARGE BRACT FOR THE 'BEAK'

13 Roll out a large piece of mid-green flowerpaste not too thinly. Cut out the large bract shape using the template on page 141 or cut freehand using plain-edge cutting wheel. Soften the edges of the shape using a foam pad and the large metal ball tool. Pinch a central vein down the length of the shape. Moisten the bract with water and then cover the beak, stretching the mid-green flowerpaste to cover the white flowerpaste beneath. Trim the flowerpaste if the shape is too large. Pinch the tip of the beak into a fine point. Stretch and smooth the bract shape at the base, down onto the main stem.

STEM BRACTS

14 Roll out more mid-green flowerpaste and cut out some pointed bract shapes, wide enough to wrap around the flower neck. Soften the edges as for the large bract. Moisten each of the bracts with fresh egg white and attach them to the main stem. Alternate the bracts at intervals down the stem, trimming off any excess length as you work. Pinch the points of the bracts and curve them slightly. Repeat this process to cover the length of stem required for your arrangement.

COLOURING

15 Use plum petal dust to tinge the edges and tips of each bract, especially where the two long edges of the larger bract join. Use foliage mixed with vine petal dusts to add colour from the tip of the large beak fading towards the main section. Add this colour to each of the smaller bracts, too. Layer Prussian blue and ultramarine craft dusts and aubergine and edelweiss petal dusts to colour the majority of the beak and the base of each of the smaller bracts. When dry, spray lightly with edible spray varnish.

LEAVES

16 These are huge! I tend to only make new growth foliage for use on cakes. Roll out a large piece of well-kneaded mid-green flowerpaste, leaving a thick ridge at the centre for the wire. Note that these leaves are quite leathery in texture. Cut out a long, pointed oval leaf shape using the large end of the plain-edge cutting wheel.

17 Insert a 20- or 18-gauge white wire moistened with fresh egg white into the ridge to support about half to three-quarters of the length of the leaf. The exact gauge will depend on the size of the leaf you are making.

18 Soften the edges of the shape using a foam pad and the large metal ball tool. Use fine angled tweezers to pinch a long, ridged central vein. Flip the leaf and use the dresden tool to draw alternating veins from the central vein down the length of the leaf to create raised veins on the upper surface.

19 Turn the leaf again and use the medium metal ball tool to hollow out the areas between the raised veins. Pinch the leaf to accentuate the central vein. Curve as required but note these leaves are flatish in form. Allow to firm up a little before colouring.

COLOURING

20 Use aubergine petal dust to catch the edges, tip and very base of the leaf. Use a large flat dusting brush to colour the main body of the leaf in layers with woodland, forest and foliage petal dusts. Allow to dry and then spray with edible spray varnish or dip into a half-glaze (see page 13). Allow to dry and then highlight the central vein with some white and vine petal dusts mixed together with isopropyl alcohol. If the highlight is too extreme, gently over-dust with a light mixture of vine and foliage petal dusts.

Gingko

Considered to be the most ancient of all living trees with fossil samples dating back to the Jurassic period, the leaves of this plant are highly decorative and useful for floral sprays for cakes. Even the fruit of the plant can add an interesting decorative edge to a floral display.

LEAVES

1 Roll out some pale green flowerpaste, leaving a thick ridge for the wire. Cut out the leaves using one of the four sizes of gingko leaf cutters or refer to the templates on page 140 and use the plain-edge cutting wheel or scalpel to cut out the shapes.

2 Insert a 28-, 26- or 24-gauge white wire moistened with fresh egg white into the central ridge to support most of the length of the leaf. The exact gauge will depend on the size of the leaf you are making. Pinch the base of the leaf firmly against the wire and work the flowerpaste down the wire to create an elongated, slightly fleshy, tapered stem. Trim off any excess as you thin the flowerpaste out. Alternatively, you could wait for the leaf to dry and then add some extra flowerpaste onto the wire, blending it into the base of the leaf and working it to create the same effect.

3 Soften the edges of the leaf with the metal ball tool and then place the leaf onto the non-stick board and work the bottom edge of the leaf with the broad end of the dresden tool, repeating the pulling/thinning process at close intervals along the edge to create a slightly frilled effect.

4 Next, place the leaf into one of the gingko leaf veiners and press firmly to texture the surface of the leaf. Remove the leaf from the veiner and pinch it down the centre to accentuate the central vein. Place it onto some dimpled foam to support the leaf as it dries slightly. Repeat to make numerous leaves in graduating sizes.

5 Dust the leaves in layers, starting with a light dusting of forest petal dust followed by foliage and an over-dusting of vine petal dusts. Add tinges to the bottom edge using a mixture of ruby and aubergine petal dusts. Allow to dry and then spray lightly with edible spray varnish.

FRUIT

6 Bend a hook in the end of a 26- or 24-gauge white wire using fine-nose pliers. Form a ball of well-kneaded pale green flowerpaste. The fruit is actually quite large, however, I have made my version slightly smaller to make it easier to use on cakes. Moisten the hook with water and insert it into the ball of flowerpaste. Work the flowerpaste into more of an oval shape and then slightly flatten both sides of the shape, pinching a gentle ridge around the edges. Pinch a little of the flowerpaste at the base of the fruit down onto the wire and work it between your finger and thumb to create an elongated thickened stem. Gently bend the stem. Allow to dry a little before dusting.

MATERIALS

Pale green flowerpaste
28-, 26-, 24- and 22-gauge white wires
Fresh egg white
Forest, foliage, vine, ruby and aubergine petal dusts
Edible spray varnish

EQUIPMENT

Non-stick rolling pin
Gingko leaf cutters (TT)
Plain-edge cutting wheel or scalpel
Metal ball tool
Non-stick board
Dresden tool
Gingko leaf veiners (SKGI or SC)
Dimpled foam
Dusting brushes
Fine-nose pliers

Monstera

Monstera deliciosa is a creeping vine native to the tropical rainforests of southern Mexico and south of Panama. Often known as the Swiss cheese plant because of the large holes in the plant's leaves, it has other fun common names connected with part of the plant's edible fibre and also its size: fruit salad plant, window leaf and my favourite, delicious monster!

LEAF

1 Roll out a large piece of well-kneaded mid-green flowerpaste, leaving a long, thick ridge for the wire. Cut out the leaf shape using one of the monstera leaf cutters or refer to the templates on page 142 and use the plain-edge cutting wheel to cut out the shapes.

2 Insert a suitable gauge of white wire moistened with fresh egg white into the thick ridge of the leaf to support about half to two-thirds of the length of the leaf. Next, place the leaf against the non-stick board with the ridged side (the back) of the leaf uppermost. Use the smooth ceramic tool to roll, thin and broaden each of the leaf sections a little.

3 Place the leaf onto the foam pad and soften the edges using the large metal ball tool. Pick up the leaf and pinch it from behind, starting at the base and working through to the tip to create a central vein and a little movement too.

4 Use a pair of angled smooth tweezers to pinch a raised central ridge vein down the leaf.

MATERIALS

Mid-green flowerpaste

22-, 20- and 18-gauge white wires

Fresh egg white

Woodland, forest, foliage, vine, aubergine and moss petal dusts

Edible spray varnish

Nile green floristry tape

COLOURING

5 It is best to dust the leaves while they are still pliable so that a good depth of colour is achieved easily without damaging the fairly fragile sections of the form. Dust in layers of woodland, forest, foliage, moss and a touch of vine petal dusts using a large flat dusting brush. Add tinges of aubergine if desired to the tip and side edges of the leaf to break up the space a little. Leave to dry and then glaze using edible spray varnish. Although the leaves are fairly shiny, it is best to build up the shine with a couple of fine layers of glaze rather than one heavy one.

6 Tape and thicken the stem using a few layers of half-width nile green floristry tape.

EQUIPMENT

Non-stick rolling pin

Monstera leaf cutters (AD)

Plain-edge cutting wheel

Non-stick board

Smooth ceramic tool

Foam pad

Large metal ball tool

Angled smooth tweezers

Large dusting brushes

Moon and sun bouquet

A very dramatic and stunning combination of white and blue crane flowers, spotted scorpion orchids, monstera foliage, eucalyptus and succulent foliage are used here to maximum effect in these complementing bouquets.

MATERIAL AND EQUIPMENT

Wire cutters or large sharp scissors

22- and 18-gauge white wires

Nile green floristry tape

Pewter tankard (optional)

Decorative paper-covered wire

FLOWERS

2 crane flowers plus one set of petals/stamen (p 44)

7 monstera leaves, in assorted sizes (p 49)

2 flapjack kalanchoe (p 89)

3 spotted scorpion orchids (p 68)

2 pale green scorpion orchids (p 68)

2 groups of gum nuts, plus foliage (p 70)

5 umbrella tree stalks (p 71)

5 gingko leaves (p 48)

PREPARATION

1 First of all strengthen/lengthen any of the flower or foliage stems that require it by taping onto extra 22- or 18-gauge white wires using half-width nile green floristry tape.

ASSEMBLY

2 Take one crane flower and then tape three monstera leaves around its neck using full-width nile green floristry tape.

3 Next, add a flapjack kalanchoe rosette where the crane flower stem and the monstera leaves join. Use the single set of crane flower petals to the left-hand side of the display to balance out the display.

4 Tape in two spotted scorpion orchids to the left-hand side of the display, then add the pale green scorpion orchid diagonally opposite to balance the shape and colour.

5 Add a group of gum nuts and their foliage and a few umbrella stalks to the edges of the bouquet to soften them. Place the bouquet into a pewter tankard supported by a ball of tangled decorative paper-covered wire.

6 Tape together the second crane flower with the remaining flowers and foliage into an informal group using full-width nile green floristry tape to secure them. Rest the spray at the base of the tankard to complete the design.

2

3

5

Painter's paradise

This vibrant two-tier cake could be used as a wedding cake or birthday cake. The painted gingko leaf side design is fairly quick to create, complementing the gingko leaves in the display. The combination of the tropical, waxy-green anthuriums, with their resemblance to a painter's palette, and the vibrant pink frangipani flowers gives a contrast in texture and colour.

MATERIALS

12.5 cm (5 in) and 20 cm (8 in) round fruitcakes placed on thin cake boards of the same size

1.4 kg (3 lb 2 oz) white almond paste

1.8 kg (4 lb) white sugarpaste

30 cm (12 in) round cake drum

Clear alcohol (Cointreau or kirsch)

Fine and broad soft green satin ribbon

Non-toxic glue stick

Cocoa butter, grated

Mug and saucer

Vine, edelweiss, moss and foliage petal dusts

EQUIPMENT

Straight-edged sugarpaste smoother

Fine paintbrushes

Food-grade plastic posy pick

Fine-nose pliers

PREPARATION

1 Cover the cakes and cake drum as described on pages 11–12. Place the large cake on top of the coated cake drum and blend the join together using the straight-edged sugarpaste smoother. Place the small cake offset on top of the larger cake using a small amount of sugarpaste softened with clear alcohol to hold it in place. Once again use the straight-edged sugarpaste smoother to blend the joins together between the two cakes. Allow to dry overnight.

2 Attach a band of fine soft green satin ribbon around the base of each cake, using a small amount of softened sugarpaste at the back of the cakes to secure the ribbon in place. Secure the broad soft green satin ribbon to the cake drum's edge using non-toxic glue.

GINGKO SIDE DESIGN

3 Melt some grated cocoa butter onto a dish above a mug filled with just-boiled water. Add some vine petal dust to the melted cocoa butter and a touch of edelweiss to create an opaque painting medium. Use a fine paintbrush to paint the leaves freehand onto the sides of the cake. Allow the first layer of colour to set before adding a touch of moss and foliage petal dusts to the painting medium. Add depth and detail veining on top of the gingko leaves to complete the design.

4 Assemble the bouquet as instructed on page 56. Insert a food-grade plastic posy pick into the top tier and insert the handle of the bouquet into it. Curve and trail the length of the bouquet around the cake. Use fine-nose pliers to reposition any of the flowers or foliage that might need a tweak to make them fit in with the shape of the cake design.

Frangipani

Frangipani (*Plumeria*) is one of the best-loved tropical plants. The flowers may be white, yellow, pink, apricot or red. The plant is named after a 12th-century Italian, famous for creating a perfume from the flowers, which were a favourite of European noble ladies, including Catherine de Medici.

MATERIALS

White and mid-green flowerpaste
28-, 26-, 24- and 22-gauge white wires
Fresh egg white
Nile green floristry tape
Daffodil, sunflower, plum, coral, edelweiss, aubergine, forest and foliage petal dusts
Edible spray varnish

EQUIPMENT

Simple leaf cutters (TT)
Non-stick rolling pin
Plain-edge cutting wheel
Foam pad
Metal ball tool
Very large rose petal veiner (SKGI)
Dresden tool
Smooth ceramic tool
Dusting brushes
Mandevilla leaf veiner (SKGI)

PETALS

1 Choose one of the simple leaf cutters (there are eight sizes in total). The size and shape of the flower varies between varieties. I prefer to squash the cutter to make a slightly narrower shape. Roll out some well-kneaded white flowerpaste, leaving a thick ridge for the wire. These flowers are fairly fleshy so don't roll the flowerpaste too thinly. Cut out the petal shape using your cutter or refer to the frangipani petal template on page 142 and use the plain-edge cutting wheel to cut out the shape.

2 Insert a 28- or 26-gauge white wire moistened with fresh egg white into the thick ridge so that it supports about a third of the length of the petal. The gauge will depend on the size of the flower you are making. Place the petal on the foam pad and soften the edge using the ball tool.

3 Texture the petal using the very large rose petal veiner. Remove from the veiner and place back onto the foam pad with the wire pointing towards you. Use the broad end of the dresden tool on the inner edge of the right-hand side of the petal to apply pressure, stroking the flowerpaste with the tool so that it creates a curled edge. Pinch the petal from the base to the tip and curve back slightly. Repeat to make five petals.

4 Quickly tape the five petals together using half-width nile green floristry tape to create a tight, spiralled shape. Use the smooth ceramic tool and your fingers to reshape the curled edge if needed.

COLOURING

5 Mix together daffodil and sunflower petal dusts. Add some colour at the base of each petal. Next, mix together plum and coral petal dusts with a touch of edelweiss. Dust the petals from the edge towards the centre. Add colour to the backs, too. There is also often a stronger aubergine-coloured sterol at the back of each petal. Allow to dry and then steam to set the colour.

LEAVES

6 Roll out some mid-green flowerpaste, leaving a thick ridge for the wire. Cut out the leaf using the plain-edge cutting wheel. Insert a 26-, 24- or 22-gauge white wire, moistened with fresh egg white, into the leaf. Soften the edge and vein using the mandevilla leaf veiner. Pinch from the base to the tip to accentuate the central vein.

7 Dust in layers with forest and foliage petal dusts. Add a tinge of aubergine. Allow to dry. Spray with edible spray varnish.

Ladder fern

There are many varieties of fern (*Nephrolepsis*). This is one of the quickest to make, however, it is fairly fragile, so care must be taken when using it in complicated arrangements and bouquets to avoid breakage.

FERN FROND

1 Roll out some well-kneaded mid-green flowerpaste onto the non-stick board. Remove the flowerpaste from the board and place over the sword fern cutter. Smooth over the flowerpaste against the cutter using your palm and then roll over the top with the non-stick rolling pin. This usually gives a cleaner cut than cutting out the shape in the conventional way against the board.

2 Carefully remove the flowerpaste from the cutter using the fine end of the dresden tool. This is a very fragile shape and the flowerpaste often gets stuck in the cutter, so a little care and patience is needed. Place the leaf onto the non-stick board and then double-frill the edges of each section of the leaf using the broad end of the dresden tool. Pull the tool against the flowerpaste onto the non-stick board at close intervals to create a tight, slightly untidy, frilled effect.

3 Place the leaf onto the foam pad and use the fine end of the dresden tool to draw a central vein down each section.

4 Tape over a length of 24-gauge white wire with quarter-width nile green floristry tape. Paint fresh egg white onto the length of the wire and then quickly insert the wire down the length of the fern. Press it in place and then flip the leaf over. Use angled tweezers to pinch the flowerpaste against the wire to secure the two together. Turn the leaf back over and pinch each section between your finger and thumb to give more movement. Leave to dry slightly before colouring.

COLOURING

5 The leaves vary in depth of colour and new growth would be a much paler, brighter green. Dust in layers with vine, foliage and forest petal dusts until you have the desired effect. Curve the length of the leaf at this stage too. Allow to dry and then spray with edible spray varnish.

MATERIALS

Mid-green flowerpaste
24-gauge white wires
Nile green floristry tape
Fresh egg white
Vine, foliage and forest petal dusts
Edible spray varnish

EQUIPMENT

Non-stick rolling pin
Non-stick board
Sword fern cutter (J)
Dresden tool
Foam pad
Fine paintbrush
Angled tweezers
Dusting brushes

Message in a bottle

A stunning combination of green anthuriums, pink frangipani flowers, gingko, piper, fern and Joseph's coat foliage have been combined here to create an interesting trailing bridal bouquet that could actually be made in cold porcelain and carried as the bridal bouquet. Here, the bouquet is displayed in an old ginger beer bottle that was in photographer Sue's props cupboard – I had bought a very modern vase to display the bouquet but somehow this old bottle held so much more charm.

MATERIALS AND EQUIPMENT

22- and 20-gauge white wires
Nile green floristry tape
Green paper-covered florist's wire
Fine-nose pliers
Wire cutters

FLOWERS AND FOLIAGE

3 green anthuriums (p 28)
5 pink frangipani flowers and
3 leaves (p 54)
3 trails of piper foliage (p 136)
3 ladder fern leaves (p 55)
5 Joseph's coat leaves (p 38)
12 gingko leaves (p 48)

PREPARATION

1 First of all strengthen and lengthen any of the flowers and foliage that might need it by taping 22- or 20-gauge white wire onto their stems with half-width nile green floristry tape. Next, take three lengths of green decorative paper-covered wire and plait them very loosely together. Twist either end to secure them together.

ASSEMBLY

2 Tape the three anthuriums together in a line using half-width nile green floristry tape. Try to point their spadix in different directions. Next, snuggle three pink frangipani flowers around the anthuriums taping them in tightly. Bend the plaited length of paper-covered florist's wire at the centre and tape the bend into the handle behind the flowers. Curve the plaits to frame the long heart shape of the bouquet, and wrap and twist the tail ends together to create a curl at the tip.

3 Add trails of piper foliage, along with a few frangipani leaves and a fern leaf to carry on building the curved shape of the bouquet. Trim off any excess wires as you work using wire cutters.

4 Continue adding more foliage – use a few Joseph's coat leaves together at the top of the bouquet and then balance them out with a couple more leaves at the bottom. Add a single fern leaf too to echo the fern at the top of the bouquet.

5 Tape the gingko leaves into several small groups using half-width nile green floristry tape. Add the groups of leaves at intervals around the top section of the bouquet. Add a couple of frangipani flowers and gingko leaves to the plaited trails, binding them around the wires tightly and neatly. Add a single fern leaf to the frangipani at the very tip of the bouquet so that it curves back up towards the main body of the bouquet. Display the bouquet in a tall slender vase or a vintage ginger beer bottle.

Flight of passion

This cake depicts the passionate relationship between the hummingbird and the pollination of many exotic flowers. Here, red passionflowers have been used to create a very dramatic and endearing design to this celebration cake that was created to celebrate my mum's 65th birthday!

MATERIALS

18 cm (7 in) round rich fruitcake placed on a thin cake board of the same size

750 g (1 lb 10 oz) white almond paste

900 g (2 lb) Champagne sugarpaste

Mug and saucer

Cocoa butter, grated

White, vine, foliage, bluegrass, hydrangea, plum and ruby petal dusts

Black, sienna, gold, sapphire and myrtle lustre dusts

Green sparkle fairy dust

Decorative beaded braid ribbon

Royal icing

Florist's Stay Soft

Tilting Perspex or metal cake stand

EQUIPMENT

Tracing or greaseproof paper

Scriber or pen that has run dry

Assorted fine paintbrushes

Non-slip mat

Fine-nose pliers

FLOWERS

3 trailing stems of red passionflowers (p 60)

PREPARATION

1 Cover the cake as described on pages 11–12. Allow to dry for several days before painting on the hummingbird design.

HUMMINGBIRD DESIGN

2 Trace the hummingbird design (see template on page 142) onto a sheet of tracing or greaseproof paper. Next, carefully scribe the design onto the surface of the cake using a scriber or a pen that has run dry.

3 Melt some grated cocoa butter onto a saucer above a mug filled with just-boiled water. Add a touch of white petal dust to the melted cocoa butter to form an opaque painting medium. Add the various coloured petal dusts to build up the colouring on the bird. Start with vine and foliage mixed together to form a light base coat. Add depth and colour variation using bluegrass and then hydrangea petal dusts. Use a mixture of plum and ruby to colour the beak. Outline and define the shape of the bird and its wing and tail feathers using a mixture of black and sienna lustre dusts. Use this mixture to paint the eyes too. You will need to allow each layer of colour to dry for 5 minutes or so before applying the next layer. Highlight the wing, tail and body feathers using gold, sapphire and myrtle lustre dusts. Allow the paintwork to dry a little more and then dust lightly with green sparkle fairy dust.

4 Use a dry paintbrush to lightly dust a mixture of gold lustre and vine petal dust around the bird, taking care not to smudge the cocoa butter paintwork.

5 Attach a band of decorative beaded braid ribbon around the base of the cake, using a small amount of royal icing at the back of the cake to secure it in place.

ASSEMBLY

6 I have used a decorative metal candle holder to display the cake but a perspex tilting stand could be used instead. Fill the candle holder with florist's Stay Soft and press to create a tilted angle. Place a small piece of non-slip mat on top of the Stay Soft and then position the cake on top.

7 Bend a hook in the end of a long trailing stem of red passion flower using fine-nose pliers and insert the wire into the Stay Soft, curving the stem around the cake. Add another flower at the front of the cake, inserting its wire into the florist's Stay Soft too. Curl and shape the plant material to create an attractive design. Arrange the third flower at the other side of the cake.

Red passionflower

There are around 500 species of passionflower and some wonderful hybrid forms too. I have based the flower pictured here on *Passiflora vitafolia*, which is a native of the rainforests of South America. The flowers are pollinated by hummingbirds and butterflies with long tongues as the complicated stamen structure can make it difficult for bees to get close to the nectar. It is this section of the flower that is the most time-consuming aspect of the flower to make.

MATERIALS

33-, 30-, 28-, 26-, 24-, 22-, 20-gauge white wires

Pale green, white, pale coral and mid-green flowerpaste

White and nile green floristry tape

Vine, sunflower, ruby, coral, African violet forest, aubergine, foliage and edelweiss white petal dusts

Isopropyl alcohol

Fresh egg white

Edible spray varnish or quarter-glaze

EQUIPMENT

Wire cutters

Plain-edge cutting wheel

Scalpel

Dusting brushes

Fine paintbrushes

Non-stick rolling pin

Grooved board

Jasmine leaf or single petal daisy cutter

Metal ball tool

Stargazer B petal veiner

Dresden tool

Briar rose leaf veiner

Hop leaf cutter (TT)

Non-stick board

Very large hydrangea leaf veiner (SKGI)

PISTIL

1 Cut three short lengths of 30-gauge white wire. Roll a small ball of pale green flowerpaste and insert a wire into it. Work the flowerpaste down the wire, leaving a rounded bead at the tip and a slender neck. Curve the shape into a lazy 'S' shape. Repeat to make three identical sections. Use the plain-edge cutting wheel to indent the underside of the bead shape on each section. Tape the three sections together using quarter-width white floristry tape.

2 Below the pistil is the ovary, which after pollination of the flower, develops into the fruit. At this flower stage the ovary is fairly small. Attach a small piece of pale green flowerpaste to the base of the pistil and form it into an oval shape.

STAMENS

3 Cut five short lengths of 33-gauge white wire. Blend a small amount of pale green flowerpaste onto a wire to create the short length of filament. Flatten the flowerpaste slightly. Repeat to make five filaments. Allow to dry a little. Next, form the

anther, shaping a small ball of pale green? flowerpaste into a sausage shape. Moisten the tip of the filament and insert it into the anther to form a 'T'-shaped stamen. Use the plain-edge cutting wheel or scalpel to mark a single line along the top length of the anther. Repeat to make five stamens. Curve the length of the filaments slightly before taping them around the ovary using quarter-width white floristry tape. Allow to dry.

4 Next, work a small amount of pale green flowerpaste down the wire below the stamens to cover about 2.5 cm (1 in) of the wire, creating a fine platform.

5 Dust this section, plus the stamen filaments, the ovary and the underside of the pistil sections with a mixture of vine and edelweiss white petal dusts. Dust the stamen anthers with sunflower petal dust. Use ruby and coral petal dusts to colour the upper surface of the three pistil sections.

6 Dilute a small amount of ruby and coral petal dusts with isopropyl alcohol and add tiny spots to the filaments and platform using a fine paintbrush.

7 Add a ball of white flowerpaste at the base of the platform and form it into a teardrop shape. Use the plain-edge cutting wheel to create a series of lines in the teardrop to represent the closed filaments at the base. Allow to dry.

8 Next, create the finer filaments, rolling several fine strands of white flowerpaste, trying to taper them into a fine point. Attach these filaments around the base using fresh egg white. You might need to hang the section upside down at this stage to allow the filaments to firm up and hold their shape. Curve the tips as you work. You will probably need between 25 and 30 of these fine sections.

9 Dust the base of the filaments with a mixture of coral and ruby petal dusts. Dilute some African violet petal dust with isopropyl alcohol and paint the tips of the filaments (this does vary between varieties – some have almost black tips, while others are pure white, and some have completely red filaments).

PETALS

10 Roll out a small amount of pale? coral flowerpaste, leaving a thick ridge for the wire – you might prefer to use a grooved board for this. Cut out the petal shape using the jasmine leaf cutter or single petal daisy cutter, or use a sharp scalpel and the template on page 142. Insert a 28-gauge white wire moistened with fresh egg white into the broader end of the shape so that the wire supports about a third of the length of the petal.

11 Soften the edge of the petal using the metal ball tool and then vein using the double-sided stargazer B petal veiner. Remove the petal from the veiner and gently pinch it from the base through to the tip to accentuate the central vein and give the shape some movement. Repeat to make five inner petals and then repeat the process with the five outer petals, but trim them slightly to create a finer shape.

12 Dust the petals with a mixture of coral and ruby petal dusts. Add extra depth to the edges with ruby petal dust. Use slightly less colour on the back of each petal. Tape the five broader petals around the base of the filaments using half-width nile green floristry tape and then position the slimmer petals slightly behind them to fill in the gaps. It is good if the flowerpaste is still pliable at this stage as it will allow you to reshape and curve the petals into shape.

13 Behind the petals there is a fleshy section. Create this by adding a ball of well-kneaded coral-coloured flowerpaste flattened tightly behind the petals. Use the plain-edge cutting wheel to divide this into ten sections.

BRACTS

14 There are three leaf-like bracts behind the flower. Roll out some pale green flowerpaste and cut out three small bract shapes using a small simple leaf cutter. Use the broad end of the dresden tool to work the edges of the bracts pulling them out at intervals to create a slightly serrated edge. Next, vein them using a briar rose leaf veiner. Pinch each bract from the base through to the tip and attach to the back of the flower using fresh egg white. Allow to dry a little, then dust with a mixture of foliage and vine green petal dust. Tinge the edges with a mixture of ruby and aubergine petal dust.

BUDS

15 Form a ball of well kneaded coral-coloured flowerpaste into a slender teardrop shape. Bend a hook in the end of a 22-gauge white wire, moisten it with fresh egg white and insert into the broad base of the shape.

16 Next, divide the surface of the bud to create five outer petals using a combination of flat angled tweezers and and your finger and thumb to pinch them into flanges/ridges. Pinch the edges of each section until they are quite fine on the edges. Twist the petals around the bud slightly to create a more spiralled formation.

17 Use a smooth ceramic tool or small celstick to mark and indent a waistline near the base of the bud to echo the rounded back of the flower. Dust as for the flower petals and then add the three bracts as described in step 14.

LEAVES

18 Roll out some mid-green flowerpaste, leaving a thick ridge down the centre for the wire. Cut out the leaf shape using the hop leaf cutter or refer to the template on page 142. Depending on the size of the leaf, insert a 26-, 24- or 22-gauge white wire moistened with fresh egg white into the thick ridge to support about half the length of the leaf.

19 Place the leaf ridge-side up against the non-stick board and work the edges slightly to create a gently serrated edge using the broad end of the dresden tool. Use the tool to pull out the edges against the board.

20 Vein using the very large double-sided hydrangea leaf veiner. Remove leaf and pinch each section from base to tip to accentuate the central vein. Repeat to make leaves in graduating sizes. Tape over each leaf stem with quarter-width nile green floristry tape.

21 Dust with layers of forest, foliage and vine petal dusts. Add a tinge of aubergine mixed with ruby to the edges. Allow to dry, then spray lightly with edible spray varnish or dip into a quarter-glaze.

FRUIT

22 Bend an open hook in the end of a length of 22-gauge white wire. Moisten the hook with fresh egg white and insert into a ball of pale green well-kneaded flowerpaste. Next, form the ball into more of an oval/egg shape. Pinch the base of the shape against the wire to secure it in place. Work some of the paste down against the wire to create a fleshier stem. Curve the stem slightly.

23 Dust with a mixture of forest, foliage and edelweiss white petal dusts. Add gentle tinges of aubergine to the tip and the base. Add white markings to the surface of the fruit using a mixture of isopropyl alcohol and edelweiss petal dust with a slight touch of foliage green just to take the extreme whiteness away a little. Use a fine paintbrush to add the random markings over the fruit. Allow to dry and spray very lightly with edible spray varnish.

24 Create the impression of dead petals to add at the base of the fruit using a few pieces of white floristry tape cut into pointed petal shapes. Stretch each of the tape petals and pinch them at the tips and at the base and then tape onto the stem of the fruit using half-width nile green floristry tape. Dust with a light mixture of cream and white petal dust. Add tinges of aubergine.

ASSEMBLY

25 Take a length of 20-gauge white wire and add a small leaf at the top using half-width nile green floristry tape. Continue to add leaves down the stem alternating their position and increasing a little in size too. Add tendrils at leaf axils. These are simply lengths of 33-gauge wire taped over with quarter-width nile green tape and curled and spiralled a little around a fine paintbrush handle. Continue adding leaves gradually introducing the buds and eventually the flowers again adding them at leaf axils. Add extra 20-gauge wire for added support and length.

Passion and drama

Here I have displayed the dramatic and eye-catching red passionflowers, fruit and foliage from the Flight of Passion cake, entwined and wrapped around a decorative wire ball. It is often nice for the recipient to keep the floral displays and use them as temporary decoration around the house for a period of time after the event.

MATERIALS AND EQUIPMENT

22- and 20-gauge white wires

Nile green floristry tape

Fine-nose pliers

Floristry scissors

Wire cutters

Decorative bronze wire ball and a small flat base

Artists' black tack

FLOWERS AND FOLIAGE

3 red passionflowers (p 60)

3 trails of passionflower foliage (p 63)

3 passionfruit (p 63)

PREPARATION

1 First of all strengthen any of the foliage, fruit and flower stems that need extra length or support by taping them onto either 22- or 20-gauge white wires using half-width nile green floristry tape. Trim off any excess using floristry scissors or wire cutters.

2 Secure the bronze-effect wire ball/sphere onto the flat base using a few small pieces of artists' black tack to hold it in place and stop it rolling around.

ASSEMBLY

3 Start by curving a long trailing stem of passionflower foliage. Use fine-nose pliers to bend it into a graceful shape. Carefully thread the stem through the gaps in the wire ball. Use a little black tack to hold the stem if required. Next, add a trail of foliage at the base of the ball to trail attractively around the right-hand side and in front of the display. These two lengths of foliage help to create a lazy 'S'-shaped arrangement.

4 Add a shorter trail of foliage to frame the side of the ball. Finally add the three red passionflowers and the passionfruit to the design, bending their stems with fine-nose pliers to angle their heads and create an attractive composition.

5 Stand back from the display and then if needed, re-adjust any of the flowers and foliage that might need a tweak using the fine-nose pliers.

Magical sensation

The intense striped markings of the scorpion orchids are a perfect match for this beautiful dark red rose. The pattern created by the umbrella tree stalks provided very simple inspiration for the painted design on this striking birthday or ruby anniversary cake.

MATERIALS

1 kg (2 lb 3 oz) white almond paste

1.5 kg (3 lb 5 oz) white sugarpaste

23 cm (9 in) heart-shaped rich fruitcake placed on a thin cake board of the same size

33 cm (13 in) heart-shaped cake drum

Vine green paste food colour

Fine and broad dark red satin ribbon

Clear alcohol (Cointreau or kirsch)

Non-toxic glue stick

Food-grade plastic posy pick

Aubergine, ruby and vine petal dusts

EQUIPMENT

Fine-nose pliers

Very fine and fine paintbrushes

FLOWERS

Magical sensation spray (p 72)

4 umbrella tree stalks (p 71)

PREPARATION

1 Colour the white sugarpaste with a little vine green paste food colour. Leave to rest a little before coating the cake and cake drum as described on pages 11–12. Attach a fine band of dark red satin ribbon around the base of the cake, using a small amount of sugarpaste softened with clear alcohol. Secure the broad dark red satin ribbon to the cake drum's edge using non-toxic glue.

2 Tape the flowers and foliage together as described on page 72. Insert the posy pick into the top of the cake and then insert the handle of the spray into it. Use fine-nose pliers to re-adjust any of the flowers that might need it to create a more pleasing effect once the flowers are on the cake.

SIDE DESIGN

3 Dilute a small amount of aubergine and ruby petal dusts with clear alcohol. Use a very fine paintbrush to create the spoke-like stems of the umbrella tree directly onto the cake and the cake drum. Next, dilute a small amount of vine petal dust and use a fine paintbrush to add a dot at the very centre of the spokes.

4 To complete the display, tuck a few extra umbrella tree stalks around the base of the cake.

Scorpion orchid

There are more than 20 species and many hybrid forms of *Arachnis* orchid, also commonly known as the scorpion orchid. These flowers make an unusual addition to the flower-maker's repertoire and can be almost any colour except blue. Petals are often spotted or striped.

COLUMN

1 Cut a short length of 26-gauge white wire. Insert it into a small ball of well-kneaded white flowerpaste. Work the ball of flowerpaste down the wire very slightly to create a short neck. Hollow out the underside of the column by pressing it gently but firmly against the rounded end of the smooth ceramic tool. This will also create a subtle ridge on the upper surface of the column.

2 Roll a tiny ball of white flowerpaste to represent the anther cap. Attach the tip of the column so that it sits in between the hollowed area and the upper surface. Use the plain-edge cutting wheel to divide the anther cap down the centre. Leave to dry.

LIP (LABELLUM)

3 Take a ball of well-kneaded pale vine green flowerpaste and form it into a teardrop shape. Next, pinch and form a short fine node at the pointed end of the teardrop and pinch out the flowerpaste around it. Place the shape against the non-stick board and roll out the flowerpaste around the node. Place the lip cutter over the flowerpaste so the node is at the base of the shape. If you are using the template on page 141, cut a hole in the template so it fits over the node.

4 Soften the edges and hollow out the inside of the tool side sections. Use fine angled tweezers to pinch a few ridges down the length of the middle section. Use the pointed end of the smooth ceramic tool to indent the area above the node to hollow it out, creating a nectary. Moisten the edges of the column with fresh egg white and attach the lip/labellum to it with the hollowed side facing the petal. Curl the edges of the two side sections back slightly and curve the very tip of the lip. Allow to set before colouring.

COLOURING

5 Dust the tip of the lip intensely with plum petal dust. Catch the curled side edges gently with colour. Add a little daffodil and sunflower petal dusts at the very centre of the lip. Use a light mixture of edelweiss and vine on the underside of the nectary area.

MATERIALS

26-gauge white wires

White and pale vine green flowerpaste

Fresh egg white

Plum, daffodil, sunflower, edelweiss, vine, aubergine, moss and foliage petal dusts

Nile green floristry tape

Isopropyl alcohol

Edible spray varnish

EQUIPMENT

Wire cutters

Smooth ceramic tool

Plain-edge cutting wheel

Non-stick board

Lip cutter

Fine angled tweezers

Non-stick rolling pin

Scorpion orchid cutter set or templates on p 141

Foam pad

Metal ball tool

Stargazer B petal veiner

Dusting brushes, including a flat dusting brush

Fine paintbrush

Fine-nose pliers

OUTER PETALS AND SEPALS

6 I think of an orchid as a figure with a head and four limbs. The dorsal is the head sepal. Roll out some pale vine green flowerpaste, leaving a thick ridge for the wire. Cut out the dorsal sepal using the straightest cutter from the set or the template on page 141 and a sharp scalpel. Insert a 26-gauge white wire moistened with fresh egg white into the petal to support a third to half its length. Pinch the flowerpaste at the base of the petal down onto the wire to secure it.

7 Place the petal onto the foam pad and soften the edges using the metal ball tool. Texture the petal using the double-sided stargazer B petal veiner. Remove petal from the veiner and pinch it back from the base through to tip to create a hollowed-out look at the back of the petal. Curve the petal forwards slightly. Allow to firm up before colouring/assembly. Repeat the process using the other cutters to create two curved wing petal shapes, turning the cutter over to create a left and right petal shape. Do the same with the leg sepal cutter. Create more of a curved bow legged shape to these two.

ASSEMBLY AND COLOURING

8 The colouring can be done before assembly or once the flower has been taped up. Start by taping the two larger curved lateral petals onto either side of the column and lip/labellum using half-width nile green floristry tape. Next, add the head/

dorsal sepal followed by the legs/lateral sepals. If the flowerpaste is still pliable, this will allow you to reshape to create a more realistic flower shape.

9 Dust the petals/sepals with a mixture of vine, a touch of daffodil and edelweiss petal dusts. To create the markings, dilute a mixture of aubergine and plum petal dusts with isopropyl alcohol and use a fine paintbrush to paint on the detail. Try not to paint the stripes too neatly. Allow to dry.

10 Mix together some more plum and aubergine petal dusts and use a flat dusting brush to over-dust the edges of the petals/sepals, bringing the colour over some of the painted stripes to calm the colour down.

11 Mix a little moss and foliage petal dusts to tinge the back of the petals. Allow to dry, then spray with edible spray varnish.

OVARY

12 Attach a ball of pale vine green flowerpaste behind the flower and work it down the stem to create a fleshy stem-like ovary. Use the plain-edge cutting wheel to mark a series of fine lines down

the length. Dust to match the petals/sepals.

BUDS

13 Using fine-nose pliers, bend a hook in the end of a 26-gauge white wire. Form a ball of pale vine green flowerpaste and insert the hooked wire moistened with fresh egg white into the base. Pinch it onto the wire to secure the two together to create a strong join. Pinch a small node/nectary at the base of the bud. Use the plain-edge cutting wheel to mark lines to give the impression of the outer sepals tightly formed around the bud. Repeat to make buds in graduating sizes.

Gum nuts

This funny name has been given to the woody seed pods of the eucalyptus tree or gum tree. There are more than 700 species of eucalyptus, mostly native to Australia. Eucalyptus are cultivated throughout the tropics and subtropics.

MATERIALS

Pale green flowerpaste

26-, 24- and 22-gauge white wires

Fresh egg white

Woodland, foliage, edelweiss, aubergine and nutkin brown petal dusts

Edible spray varnish

Nile green floristry tape

EQUIPMENT

Smooth ceramic tool

Small ball tool

Fine celstick

Fine-nose pliers

Non-stick rolling pin

Gum leaf cutters

Plain-edge cutting wheel

Foam pad

Dusting brushes

GUM NUTS

1 Form a ball of well-kneaded pale green flowerpaste into a teardrop shape. Use the pointed end of the smooth ceramic tool to open up the pointed end of the shape, then use the rounded end of the tool to open up the shape a little more. Use the small ball tool to hollow out the inner rim of the shape. To create a slight waist, insert the fine celstick into the centre and squeeze the shape against it. You may need to re-hollow the rim and re-form the waist until the desired shape is achieved.

2 Bend an open hook in the end of a 24- or 22-gauge white wire, depending on the size of gum nut. Moisten the hook with fresh egg white and pull the wire through the centre of the pod, embedding the hook into the fleshier area. Pinch the flowerpaste at the base of the pod and work it down onto the wire. Work the flowerpaste with your finger and thumb to create a fine neck. Curve the stem. Allow to firm up a little before dusting.

LEAVES

3 Roll out some well-kneaded pale green flowerpaste, leaving a thick ridge for the wire. Use one of the gum leaf cutters or refer to the template on page 142 and use the plain-edge cutting wheel to cut out the leaf shape. Insert a 26- or 24-gauge white wire moistened with fresh egg white into the thick ridge to support about half the length of the leaf. Pinch the base of the leaf down onto the wire then work the flowerpaste between finger and thumb to create a fine stem coating.

4 Place the leaf on the foam pad and soften the edge using the ball tool. Use the plain-edge cutting wheel to draw a central vein down the leaf and then use the small wheel to mark some finer side veins tapering out from the central vein. Pinch the leaf from base to tip to shape it and define the central vein. Allow to firm before colouring. Repeat to make leaves in various sizes.

COLOURING

5 Dust the leaves with a mixture of woodland, foliage and edelweiss petal dusts. Catch the edges with a touch of aubergine. Allow to dry and then spray very lightly with edible spray varnish.

6 Dust the gum nut pods with the same mixture, adding aubergine and nutkin brown into the very heart and very edges of the pod and slightly at the base. Allow to dry and spray lightly with edible spray varnish. Tape over each leaf stem with quarter-width nile green floristry tape. Tape the leaves alternating down the length of a 22-gauge white wire with half-width nile green tape. Add the gum nuts in clusters from the leaf axils.

Umbrella tree stalks

I first saw these wonderful things being used in an Australian floristry book. I had no idea what they were! It turns out they are the stalks of the Australian umbrella tree, the leaves removed by the florist, to leave these exciting firework-style stalks. They can be very pale green or, as I prefer, tinged with a dark red. They are very simple to make and add an instant touch of drama.

STALKS

1 The number of stems per stalk varies, with as few as five stems creating a complete stalk. Cut several 33-gauge white wires into four sections using wire cutters.

2 Roll a very small ball of well-kneaded pale green flowerpaste. Wrap the flowerpaste around a short length of wire and work it to the tip of the wire to create the required stalk length. Keep working the flowerpaste firmly between your finger and thumb, removing the excess flowerpaste at the tip of the wire. Place the stalk between your palms and roll it firmly to create a smoother finish. Repeat to make several stalks. Don't worry about making them all the same length as they vary in length a little on one stalk.

ASSEMBLY AND COLOURING

3 Use fine-nose pliers to bend each wire at the base of the stalk as you tape them together using half-width nile green floristry tape. Tape together several stems to create a stalk. Use the side of a pair of scissors to rub against the tape to smooth it and leave a slight shine. Trim any of the sections that need shortening.

4 Roll a very tiny ball of pale green flowerpaste and stick it into the very centre where each of the stems join together. Use the broad end of the dresden tool to indent the centre of the ball and bond it to the stalk.

5 Dust the undersides and the upper side at the very centre with a mixture of vine, a touch of daffodil and a touch of edelweiss petal dusts. Use a mixture of plum, ruby and aubergine to dust the upper surface of each section, leaving the very heart of the stalk a bright green. Allow to dry and then spray with edible spray varnish.

MATERIALS

33-gauge white wires
Pale green flowerpaste
Nile green floristry tape
Vine, daffodil, edelweiss, plum, ruby and aubergine petal dusts
Edible spray varnish

EQUIPMENT

Wire cutters
Fine-nose pliers
Non-stick rolling pin
Scissors
Dresden tool
Dusting brushes

Magical sensation spray

I love working with dark, rich red flowers. Here, a dark red rose forms the focal point, with the wonderfully vibrant striped scorpion orchids and dark red-tinged anthuriums adding an instant tropical sensation. The spiky groups of red umbrella tree stalks add an extra touch of drama, creating almost a firework effect at the edges of the spray.

MATERIALS

22-gauge white wires

Nile green floristry tape

EQUIPMENT

Wire cutters

Decorative vase (optional)

FLOWERS

1 dark red rose (p 100)

3 scorpion orchids (p 68)

2 flamingo flowers (p 29)

1 regular anthurium (p 28)

5 sprigs of ylang-ylang berries (p 23)

3 senecio leaves (p 113)

3 groups of gum nuts plus foliage (p 70)

7 umbrella tree stalks (p 71)

PREPARATION

1 Add extra length or strength to any of the components by taping them onto 22-gauge white wire using half-width nile green floristry tape.

ASSEMBLY

2 Take the dark red rose and place the three striped scorpion orchids around it. Tape their stems together using half-width nile green floristry tape. Angle their faces in different directions – there is nothing worse than having them all pointing the same way. Trim off any excess wires using wire cutters.

3 Next, tape the two red-tinged flamingo anthuriums plus one regular anthurium opposite each other on either side of the rose to fill some space in between the orchids. Add the sprigs of ylang-ylang berries to add extra length to the spray. The piece at the tip of the spray should be longer than the piece at the back. Remember that when forming sprays, a good guideline is to divide the length into thirds: two-thirds from the tip of the spray to the focal point and the remaining third from the focal point to the top of the spray.

4 Use the senecio leaves and the gum nuts and their foliage to fill in the remaining gaps around the edges of the spray.

5 Finally add the umbrella tree stalks around the edges of the spray. Display the spray on a cake or as pictured here in a suitable container. Add a few umbrella stalks at the base of the display.

2

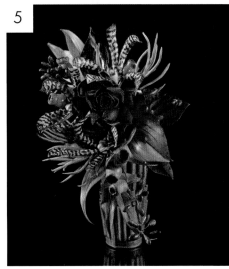

Tranquil waters

The crystal-filled glass cake stand lends an almost floating, tranquil platform for this pretty celebration cake that would be suitable for a small birthday celebration or anniversary. A single blue water lily creates a very calm vibe to this design.

MATERIALS

15 cm (6 in) round fruitcake placed on a thin cake board of the same size

350 g (12 oz) white almond paste

350 g (12 oz) white sugarpaste

Crystal-filled glass cake stand (or similar)

Purple organza ribbon

Clear alcohol (Cointreau or kirsh)

Silver organza ribbon

Food-grade plastic posy pick

EQUIPMENT

Straight-sided sugarpaste smoother

Fine-nose pliers

FLOWERS

Tranquil waters spray (p 82)

PREPARATION

1 Coat the cake as described on pages 11–12. Position it on top of the glass cake stand and use the straight-sided sugarpaste smoother to blend and neaten the join between the cake and the stand.

2 Attach a band of purple organza ribbon around the base of the cake, using a small amount of sugarpaste softened with clear alcohol to hold it in place. Layer a length of silver organza ribbon over the top. Leave to dry.

3 Assemble the blue water lily spray as described on page 82. Insert the posy pick into the top surface of the cake and insert the handle of the spray into it. Use fine-nose pliers to reposition any of the flowers and leaves that require it to create a more pleasing connection between the cake and the floral display.

Devil's ivy

These wonderful silver-spotted, long, heart-shaped leaves are great to trail and add detail at the same time to bouquets and arrangements. There are about 400 species of philodendron with the shape, size and colour varying quite substantially between each one.

MATERIALS

Mid-green flowerpaste

26-, 24-, 22- and 20-gauge white wires

Fresh egg white

Foliage, forest, edelweiss and aubergine petal dusts

Myrtle bridal satin dust

Isopropyl alcohol

Nile green floristry tape

Edible spray varnish

EQUIPMENT

Non-stick rolling pin

Heart-shaped leaf cutters

Plain-edge cutting wheel

Foam pad

Large metal ball tool

Dimpled foam or crumpled kitchen paper

Dusting brushes

Fine paintbrushes

1 Roll out some mid-green flowerpaste not too thinly, leaving a thicker area at the centre to hold the wire. Cut out the leaf shape using one of the heart-shaped leaf cutters or refer to the devil's ivy template on page 141 and use the plain-edge cutting wheel to cut out the shape.

2 Insert a 26-, 24- or 22-gauge white wire moistened with fresh egg white into the thick ridge to support about half the length of the leaf. Place the leaf onto the foam pad or onto your palm and soften the edge using a rolling action with the large metal ball tool.

3 Pinch the leaf from the base to the tip to create a central vein and give the leaf some movement at the same time. Allow to dry over some dimpled foam or crumpled kitchen paper to help give the leaf a little support and shape. Repeat to make leaves in graduating sizes.

COLOURING AND ASSEMBLY

4 Dust the leaves with a mixture of foliage, forest and edelweiss petal dusts. Dilute some myrtle bridal satin dust with isopropyl alcohol and paint a series of irregular-sized dots and then use the brush to catch the edge of the leaf to create a border around the outside. Add tinges of aubergine to the edges of each leaf.

5 Tape over each stem with half-width nile green floristry tape. Start taping a trailing stem together, starting with a small leaf on the end of a 22- or 20-gauge white wire using half-width nile green floristry tape. Add the other leaves so that they alternate down the stem, then gradually working with full-width floristry tape to create fleshier stems as the leaves increase in size. Bend the length of the main stem to create an attractive bend and curve. Spray lightly with edible spray varnish.

Blue Egyptian water lily

This beautiful purple-blue water lily is a native to the river Nile and other areas of East Africa. The flowers have been used since ancient times to produce perfumes and have also been used in aromatherapy. Recent studies have shown that *Nymphaea caerulea* has mild psycho-active properties. It may have been used in ancient Egypt and by certain South American cultures as a sacrament. In modern culture, the flowers are often used to create a tea and to flavour wine and Martini cocktails.

MATERIALS

33-, 26-, 24-, 22- and 20-gauge white wires
Pale yellow, white and mid-green flowerpaste
Fresh egg white
Sunflower, plum, African violet, vine, white, foliage, forest and aubergine petal dusts
Nile green floristry tape
Isopropyl alcohol
Edible spray varnish

EQUIPMENT

Fine-nose pliers
Non-stick rolling pin
Medium and large metal ball tool
Dusting brushes
Wire cutters
Non-stick board
Medium paintbrush
Sage leaf cutters (TT852, 855)
Foam pad
Stargazer B or wide amaryllis petal veiner (SKGI)
Dimpled foam or kitchen ring former (p 8)
Plain-edge cutting wheel
Large circle cutter
Fine scissors
Very large nasturtium leaf veiner (SKGI)

CENTRE

1 The main wire for the centre needs to be formed into a ski stick shape. Bend an open hook in the end of a 22-gauge white wire using fine-nose pliers. Next, press the hook against the main length of wire. Now hold the hook at the centre using fine-nose pliers and bend it to form a halo or ski stick shape.

2 Roll a ball of well-kneaded pale yellow flowerpaste. Moisten the hooked wire with fresh egg white and push it into the base of the ball shape. Pinch the flowerpaste firmly around the hook and form the base into a slightly pointed shape.

3 Use the medium metal ball tool to hollow out the upper surface of the shape. Leave to firm up a little before dusting with sunflower petal dust.

STAMENS

4 Cut several short lengths of 33-gauge white wire using wire cutters. Attach a tiny ball of pale yellow flowerpaste onto one of the wires and blend it against the wire using your finger and thumb to coat about 2.5 cm (1 in) of the wire. Work the tip into a fine point. Next, flatten the shape against the non-stick board using the flat side of one of the petal veiners.

5 Pick the shape off the board and pinch it from the base through to the tip to give a little more shape. Curve the tip to represent the anther. Repeat to make about 25 to 30 stamens for each flower.

ASSEMBLY AND COLOURING

6 It is best to tape the stamens around the dried centre before they have a chance to dry so that a little reshaping to the anthers can be done easily. Tape the stamens tightly at first around the sides of the dried centre using half-width nile green floristry tape.

7 Dust the stamens with sunflower petal dust. You might prefer to do this prior to taping them onto the centre. Next, dilute some plum and African violet petal dusts mixed with isopropyl alcohol. Use a medium paintbrush to apply the colour to the tips of each of the stamens. Allow to dry and then glaze with edible spray varnish. Place to one side until required.

PETALS

8 Roll out some well-kneaded white flowerpaste, leaving a tapered thick ridge for the wire – this is quite a large-petalled flower so don't roll the flowerpaste too fine. Cut out a petal shape using the smallest of the sage leaf cutters or refer to the water lily template on page 140.

9 Insert a 26-gauge white wire moistened with fresh egg white into the thick ridge of the petal to support about a third to half the length of the petal. Pinch the flowerpaste slightly at the base down onto the wire to create a slightly more elongated shape.

10 Place the petal onto the foam pad or onto your palm and soften the edges using the metal ball tool, using a rolling and not a rubbing action. Try not to frill the edges you are just trying to remove the harsh cut edge from the petal.

11 Texture the surface of the petal using the double-sided stargazer B or wide amaryllis petal veiner. The latter has stronger veins so it will depend on the effect you prefer. Remove the petal from the veiner and pinch it gently from the base to the tip to create a subtle central vein. Hollow the length of the petal gently to encourage a curved shape. Place the petal onto dimpled foam or into a homemade paper ring former. Repeat to make five petals the same size.

12 Next, increase the size of the cutter to make ten larger petals. Repeat the above process using a 26- or perhaps even a 24-gauge white wire to support each petal.

13 Dust each petal back and front from the edges towards the base with African violet petal dust. Leave the base of each petal slightly paler. Dust the base of each petal with a light mixture of vine and white petal dusts.

14 Dust the back outer five petals with a mixture of foliage and forest petal dusts to create a broad streak of colour down the centre of each.

15 Tape the five smaller petals around the stamen centre using half-width nile green floristry tape. If the petals are still pliable, then this will enable you to bend and reshape them slightly if needed. Next, tape five slightly larger petals to fit in the gaps left by the first five petals. Finally, add the remaining five petals to complete the flower. Allow the flower to dry and then hold over a jet of steam from the kettle or use a clothes steamer to set the colour and leave a slight shine – be careful not to hold the flower in the steam for too long as this will result in a very shiny finish or worse still a sticky mess!

BUDS

16 Take a large ball of well-kneaded white flowerpaste and form it into a large cone shape. Tape over a 20-gauge white wire with half-width nile green floristry tape and bend a large hook in the end using fine-nose pliers. Moisten the hook with fresh egg white and insert it into the broad end of the cone of flowerpaste. Divide the surface of the cone into five sections using the plain-edge cutting wheel to represent the outer petals of the bud. Gently pinch each petal down the centre using your finger and thumb to create a subtle ridged effect.

17 To make a larger bud, repeat the above process adding five softened and veined unwired small petals over the cone using a little fresh egg white to secure them in place. Allow to dry and then dust as for the outer petals of the flower.

LILY PAD/LEAF

18 Roll out some well-kneaded mid-green flowerpaste, leaving a thick ridge for the wire. Cut out the leaf shape using the large circle cutter.

19 Use a pair of fine scissors to cut out a slender 'V'-shape from the base of the leaf. Insert a 22- or 20-gauge white wire moistened with fresh egg white into the thick ridge to support quite a bit of the length of the leaf.

20 Soften the edges using the large metal ball tool and then vein using the very large nasturtium leaf veiner, pressing firmly to create strong veins on the leaf. Remove the leaf from the veiner, then allow it to firm up a bit, drying it on a piece of dimpled foam or in a kitchen paper ring.

21 Dust the back and edges of the leaf with a mixture of plum and aubergine petal dusts. Dust the upper surface with forest and then lots of foliage petal dusts. Allow to dry and then glaze lightly with edible spray varnish. Bend the wire at the back of the leaf to create the plant's characteristic floating lily pads. Tape over the wire several times with half-width nile green floristry tape.

Tuberose

The tuberose (*Polianthes tuberose*) is thought to have originated in Mexico, although it is grown and used extensively in other countries. I have given instructions for both single and double forms.

MATERIALS

Small, white seed-head stamens

Hi-tack non-toxic craft glue

28-, 26-, 24- and 18-gauge white wires

Sunflower, daffodil, vine, moss, plum, edelweiss and foliage petal dusts

White and pale green flowerpaste

Fresh egg white

Nile green floristry tape

Plastic food bag

EQUIPMENT

Wire cutters

Dusting brushes

Non-stick rolling pin

Six-petal pointed blossom cutters (OP N1, 2, 3)

Foam pad

Medium and small metal ball tools

Plain-edge cutting wheel or dresden tool

Non-stick board

Smooth ceramic tool or celstick

Dried sweetcorn husk veiner

STAMENS

1 Take three small, white seed-head stamens and glue them together from the centre, working the glue towards the tips at either end. Try not to use too much glue as this will take too long to dry and create too much bulk. Allow the glue to dry and then cut the stamens in half. Trim them so that they are quite short. Apply a little more glue and attach to the end of a 24-gauge white wire. Allow to dry. Dust the tips with a mixture of sunflower and daffodil petal dusts. Dust the base of the stamens with vine petal dust.

FIRST AND SECOND LAYER OF PETALS FOR THE DOUBLE FLOWER

2 Roll out some well-kneaded white flowerpaste, leaving a raised pimple at the centre. Cut out a flower shape using the smallest six-petal pointed blossom cutter. Place the shape onto a foam pad and soften the edges using the medium metal ball tool. Next, hollow the length of each petal using the small ball tool.

3 Add fine veins to each petal using the small end of the plain-edge cutting wheel or the fine end of the dresden tool.

4 Moisten the base of the stamens with fresh egg white and thread the wire through the centre of the flower shape. Pinch the pimple behind the flower to secure it in place and push the petals upwards to create a tight centre. Allow to dry. Repeat the process to create the second layer of petals, but this time using the slightly larger six-petal pointed blossom cutter. Attach the shape onto the back of the first layer, positioning the petals over joins in the first layer. Allow to dry.

THIRD LAYER FOR THE DOUBLE FLOWER (OR METHOD FOR THE SINGLE FORM)

5 These instructions apply to the outer layer of the double tuberose, as well as being the complete method for the single variety. Form a ball of well-kneaded white

flowerpaste into a long sausage. Pinch out one end of the shape to form a wizard's hat shape. Place the flat part of the 'hat' against the non-stick board and roll out the 'brim' using the smooth ceramic tool or celstick, remembering the flower is quite fleshy.

6 Cut out the flower shape using the largest of the six-petal pointed blossom cutters. Rub your thumb over the edge to get rid of any rough edges.

7 Remove the flower from the cutter and place it face-down on the foam pad. Soften the edges of each petal gently. Use the metal ball tool to hollow the upper side of each petal for an opening flower and the back of each petal for a fully open flower. Add a few fine veins to each petal as before.

8 Open up the centre of the flower using the pointed end of the celstick or smooth ceramic tool. Moisten the back of the wired flower with fresh egg white and thread the wire through the centre of the outer flower so that the petals fill the spaces in the previous layer. Pinch the tips of the petals slightly and curl some or all of them back. If you are making the single form, thread the wired stamens through the centre instead.

9 Thin down the back of the flower between your finger and thumb, and pinch off any excess flowerpaste if needed. Use the plain-edge cutting wheel to mark six lines on the back of the flower, following the indent in between each petal. Add some finer lines in-between these divisions too. Curve the back gracefully.

BUDS

10 Form a ball of well-kneaded white flowerpaste into a cone shape. Insert a hooked 28- or 26-gauge white wire moistened with fresh egg white into the broad end. The gauge of wire will depend on the size of the bud you are making.

11 Work the flowerpaste at the base of the bud to create a more slender neck shape. Divide the upper section of the bud into three sections to represent the outer petals. Next, pinch each section gently between your finger and thumb to create a subtle ridge.

12 Use the plain-edge cutting wheel to divide and vein the surface of the bud as for the flower. Repeat to make buds in graduating sizes, remembering that they are in pairs down the stem.

BRACTS

13 To each pair of buds and flowers there is a single bract attached where they join the main stem. They can be created quickly with nile green floristry tape cut into a pointed bract shape or with flowerpaste. Roll out some pale green flowerpaste, leaving a ridge down the centre. Use the plain-edge cutting wheel to cut out freehand pointed arrow-shaped bracts in graduating sizes.

14 Soften the edges and then texture using the dried sweetcorn husk veiner. Cut out as many bracts as required and cover with a plastic food bag to stop them drying out.

ASSEMBLY AND COLOURING

15 Tape two small buds onto the end an 18-gauge white wire using half-width nile green floristry tape. Thicken the stem with a strip of kitchen paper wrapped around the wire and taped over with nile green floristry tape. Attach a small bract at the base of the buds using a little fresh egg white to secure it. Add the next two buds plus a bract. Continue this method until you have added all the buds and flowers in pairs down the stem.

16 Dust the backs of the flower and buds with vine petal dust and then add a little more depth using a mixture of daffodil and moss on top. Use this colour on the tips of the smaller buds too. Mix together plum and edelweiss petal dusts. Tinge the buds gently and add a little to the back of each flower too. Dust the bracts with a mixture of vine, moss and a touch of foliage. Allow to dry and then hold over a jet of steam to set the colour and leave a slightly waxy finish.

Tranquil waters spray

A gentle colour combination of a single blue water lily, white tuberoses and soft-green assorted foliage help to create a very tranquil feel to this pretty spray of flowers.

MATERIALS

22- and 20-guage white wires

Nile green floristry tape

EQUIPMENT

Fine-nose pliers

Decorative silver paper-covered wire

Wire cutters or florist's scissors

FLOWERS

3 trailing stems of piper (p 136)

1 blue Egyptian water lily, plus foliage (p 77)

1 group of King tillandsia leaves (page 103)

3 trailing stems of devil's ivy (p 76)

5 gingko leaves (p 48)

3 stems of tuberose (p 80)

PREPARATION

1 Elongate and strengthen any of the stems that require it by taping them onto 22- or 20-gauge white wires using half-width nile green floristry tape.

ASSEMBLY

2 Tape the three trailing stems of piper foliage behind the blue water lily using half-width nile green floristry tape. Curve the stems to create a relaxed 'S'-shaped spray.

3 Continue adding more foliage around the water lily, starting with a group of tillandsia foliage to the left-hand side of the spray. Add a few trails of devil's ivy and then fill in the gaps with the gingko leaves.

4 Next, add two stems of tuberoses and curve their stems to follow the line of the relaxed 'S'-shape of the spray. Add the third shorter stem to the left-hand side of the spray to balance the form a little more.

5 Finally, add loops and curled trails of decorative silver paper-covered wire, taping them tightly in place with half-width nile green floristry tape. Trim off any excess wire using wire cutters or florist's scissors as you go. Use fine-nose pliers to bend and reposition any of the flowers and leaves to create a more relaxed end result.

2

3

African winds

An intense colour combination gives this stunning two-tier wedding cake an instant hot and exotic vibe. Although the bird of paradise flowers dominate the design, it is the addition of the brightly coloured orange *zantedeschia* and coral ixia flowers, combined with hot pink cordyline leaves, that really give the design its maximum impact.

MATERIALS

15 cm (6 in) and 23 cm (9 in) round fruitcakes placed on thin cake boards of the same size

1.4 kg (3 lb 2 oz) white almond paste

1.8 kg (4 lb) white sugarpaste

33 cm (13 in) round cake drum

Fine and broad green satin ribbon

Clear alcohol (Cointreau or kirsch)

Non-toxic glue stick

Coral, white, ruby, vine and foliage petal dusts

EQUIPMENT

Straight-edged sugarpaste smoother

Fine paintbrush

Large food-grade plastic posy pick

Fine-nose pliers

FLOWERS

Bird of paradise bouquet (p 90)

2 trailing stems of piper foliage (p 136)

PREPARATION

1 Cover the cakes and cake drum as described on pages 11–13. Place the small cake on top of the large cake and blend the join between them using the straight-edged sugarpaste smoother. Attach a band of fine green satin ribbon around the base of each cake, using a little sugarpaste softened with clear alcohol to secure it in place. Secure the broad green satin ribbon to the edge of the board using non-toxic glue.

SIDE DESIGN

2 Paint a series of berries in graduating sizes onto the surface of both cakes and the drum using coral and a touch of white petal dusts diluted with clear alcohol. Add depth to each berry adding a little ruby petal dust to the mixture. Mix vine and foliage petal dusts diluted with clear alcohol to paint a fine connecting main stem to the berries.

3 Assemble the bouquet as described on page 90. Insert a large plastic posy pick into the top tier and position the handle of the bouquet into it. Use fine-nose pliers to re-adjust and curve the flower and foliage stems to create a more relaxed display. Balance the design by placing the two trails of piper foliage against the cake drum.

Bird of paradise

The method for making the more common orange *Strelitzia reginae* is basically the same as that used for the white crane flower on page 44. The shape of the beak is more slender and there is the obvious colour variation too. Below is the extra information you will need to make this wonderful flower.

see materials and equipment for White crane flower, p 46

MATERIALS

Purple and orange craft dusts (SF)
Edible spray varnish
White, tangerine, plum, fuchsia, aubergine, forest, foliage and edelweiss petal dusts
White floristry tape

EQUIPMENT

Large dusting brushes

Plus, see materials and equipment for White crane flower, p 46

STAMENS

1 There is one stamen to three petals. Follow the instructions for the white crane flower on page 46. While the stamen is still pliable, dust it with purple craft dust to create a fairly intense purple-blue stamen. Fade the colour slightly towards the very tip of the arrow head. Spray lightly with edible spray varnish. Dust the tip of the stamen heavily with white petal dust to represent the pollen.

PETALS

2 There are two large and one small petal to each stamen. Dust the petals as soon as they are made so that the colour sticks well and gives a good, strong colour. Use tangerine petal dust or orange craft dust and scrub the colour onto the petals leaving the base white. Tape the two large petals together using half-width white floristry tape. Add a stamen and then the small petal. This makes one section of the flower. You will need about two or three sections at least. Spray with edible spray varnish to give a glossy finish.

ASSEMBLY AND BEAK

3 Tape the petal sections together as instructed on page 45–46 using white floristry tape. Create the beak in the same way but remember to make it straighter and more slender in form than that used in the white crane flower.

COLOURING

4 Mix together plum and fuchsia petal dusts. Use a flat dusting brush to colour the edges of each bract and the join along the top edge of the beak too. Over-dust the edges slightly with aubergine petal dust. Use forest and foliage petal dusts to colour the main areas of the beak and bracts. Use edelweiss heavily over the top and then steam or spray lightly with edible spray varnish.

Zantedeschia

A native of South Africa, this wonderful plant is grown worldwide and used extensively by florists for arrangements and bridal bouquets. Though often known as the calla or arum lily, it does not belong to any of these families and should be called by its proper name *Zantedeschia*. The plants have been cultivated in Europe since 1687. The colour variation is huge, including white, yellow, pink, orange, green, red, burgundy and almost black.

MATERIALS

18-gauge white wire

Pale melon flowerpaste

Aubergine, coral, tangerine, plum, vine and foliage petal dusts

Edible spray varnish

Fresh egg white

Kitchen paper

Nile green floristry tape

EQUIPMENT

Nutmeg grater

Dusting brushes

Non-stick rolling pin

Spathe cutter (AD)

Plain-edge cutting wheel

Foam pad

Large metal ball tool

Extra wide amaryllis petal veiner (SKGI)

Dresden tool

SPADIX

1 Insert an 18-gauge white wire into a medium-size ball of well-kneaded pale melon flowerpaste. Work the flowerpaste down the wire to a length of about 4 cm (1¾ in). Smooth the shape between your palms and trim off any excess. Next, texture the surface by rolling the spadix against a nutmeg grater. Attach a ball of flowerpaste at the base of the spadix to give more padding when the spathe is attached.

2 Dust the spadix with aubergine petal dust. Allow to dry and spray lightly with edible spray varnish.

SPATHE

3 Roll out some pale melon flowerpaste, taking care not to roll the paste too fine. Cut out the spathe using the spathe cutter or refer to the template on page 142 and use the plain-edge cutting wheel to cut out the shape. Place the spathe onto the foam pad and soften the edges using the large metal ball tool. Vein the spathe using the double-sided extra wide amaryllis petal veiner. Place back onto the foam pad and add a few extra central veins down the length of the spathe using the fine end of the dresden tool.

4 Moisten the base of the spathe with fresh egg white and then place the spadix on either the left or right side (they curl both ways even on the same plant). Next, roll the two together to form the characteristic trumpet shape. Curl back the edges using your finger and thumb, and pinch and curl the very tip into a fine point. You will need to hang the flower upside down and keep going back to curl and keep the shape in check until the flower is firm enough to hold its own weight.

5 Thicken the stem with strips of kitchen paper wrapped around the wire and taped over with full-width nile green floristry tape.

COLOURING

6 The flower pictured here was dusted with a mixture of coral and tangerine petal dusts with an over-dusting of plum petal dust. Add tinges of vine mixed with foliage to the very tip, base and back of the flower. Once the flower is dry, steam it or spray lightly with edible spray varnish.

Ixia

This flower is also known as the wandflower or the corn lily from South Africa. There are over 40 species of this plant, with a huge variation in colour, including a wonderful green-petalled species. The name wandflower seems most apt as it does look like a wand with stars.

MATERIALS

White flowerpaste

33-, 30-, 28-, 26-, 24- and 22-gauge white wires

Coral, plum, ruby, sunflower and aubergine petal dusts

Nile green floristry tape

Fine white stamens (optional)

Non-toxic glue stick

White seed-head or freesia stamens

Isopropyl alcohol

EQUIPMENT

Plain-edge cutting wheel

Dusting brushes

Fine-nose pliers

Non-stick rolling pin

Small ruscus leaf cutter (TT)

Stargazer B petal veiner

Medium metal ball tool

Fine paintbrush

BUDS

1 Form a small ball of white flowerpaste into a cone shape. Depending on the size of the bud, insert a hooked 33-, 30- or 28-gauge white wire moistened with fresh egg white into the base of the cone. Work the flowerpaste down the wire slightly to create a more pointed base. Divide the bud into three to represent the outer petals using the plain-edge cutting wheel. Repeat to make buds in graduating sizes. Dust the buds with a mixture of coral and a touch of plum petal dusts. Tinge the tips with ruby petal dust. Tape over each stem with quarter-width nile green floristry tape.

PISTIL (OPTIONAL)

2 Cut the tips off three fine white stamens and glue them together with non-toxic glue, leaving a little at the ends unglued to curl back slightly. I mostly omit this, as it is very time-consuming.

STAMENS

3 Cut the tips off three white seed-head or freesia stamens and attach tiny pieces of white flowerpaste to the end of each and work the flowerpaste into a fine slender anther shape. Allow to dry and dust with sunflower petal dust. Attach the stamens and the pistil onto the end of a 28-gauge white wire using non-toxic glue, keeping them fairly short.

PETALS

4 Roll out some white flowerpaste thinly, leaving a thick ridge for the wire. Cut out the petal shape using the small ruscus leaf cutter. Insert a 33- or 30-gauge white wire moistened with fresh egg white into the thick ridge to support about a third of its length.

5 Soften the edges and then vein using the stargazer B petal veiner. Next, hollow the petal using the medium metal ball tool. Repeat to make six petals. Pinch the base and tip of each petal to create a more pointed petal shape.

COLOURING AND ASSEMBLY

6 Dust the petals to match the buds and then tape three petals around the stamens using quarter-width nile green floristry tape followed by the remaining three. Next, add a dark 'eye' to the flower using some aubergine petal dust diluted with a little isopropyl alcohol, colouring the very base of each petal on the back and front. Add this colouring to the base of each bud too.

7 Start taping the buds onto a 26-gauge white wire, increasing the bud sizes as you work down the stem. Introduce a 24- or 22-gauge white wire as you work down the stem to give more support. Introduce the flowers at the base of the stem. Curve the length of the stem gracefully.

Flapjack kalanchoe

These wonderful succulents belong to the *Kalanchoe* family. There are over 125 species in this family, with many of them producing pretty flowers. Other common names include desert cabbage and paddle plant. I love how fleshy the leaves of the Flapjack kalanchoe are. They fill space and provide interest and character to flower arrangements. They are made freehand and with no veiners, so they are quick to make and perfect for the novice sugarcrafter.

LEAVES

1 Roll a ball of well-kneaded pale green flowerpaste. Form it into a cone shape and insert a 26-, 24- or 22-gauge white wire moistened with fresh egg white into the finer end of the cone. The exact wire gauge you use will depend on the size of leaf you are making.

2 Next, flatten the shape using your fingers and thumb, pinching a thinned-out ridge along the top end of the leaf, which will help create more of a fan-shaped formation.

3 Press the leaf between your palms to pick up some palm-print veined texture to the leaf. Pinch the leaf at the base and curve and bend the top edge slightly to give a little more movement. Use a large metal ball tool to hollow out the centre of each leaf slightly. Repeat to make numerous leaves in graduating sizes.

ASSEMBLY AND COLOURING

4 Tape two of the smaller leaves together using Nile green floristry tape before the flowerpaste dries out and they can snuggle tightly together. Continue adding leaves around two central leaves using half-width nile green floristry tape until the required size of succulent is created.

5 Dust the base of each leaf on the back and front with a mixture of foliage, woodland and edelweiss petal dusts. Catch the top edges with a mixture of plum, ruby and coral petal dusts. Over-dust with aubergine. Allow to dry and then spray lightly with edible spray varnish.

MATERIALS

Pale green flowerpaste
26-, 24- and 22-gauge white wires
Fresh egg white
Nile green floristry tape
Foliage, woodland, edelweiss, plum, ruby, coral and aubergine petal dusts
Edible spray varnish

EQUIPMENT

Non-stick rolling pin
Large metal ball tool
Large flat dusting brushes

Bird of paradise bouquet

I love working with intense colours and here is a perfect example of that! Bright orange, cool blue and hot pink are all combined in this tropical bouquet of flowers. Commercial floristry rules that the number of flowers used should be in odd numbers, however, creative flower arranging and Japanese ikebana allows the use of even numbers too. Here I have used one-and-a-half bird of paradise flowers.

MATERIALS

22-, 20- and 18-gauge white wires

Nile green floristry tape

EQUIPMENT

Wire cutters

Fine-nose pliers

Slender black frosted glass vase

FLOWERS

1 orange bird of paradise, plus two sets of petals/stamens (p 86)

3 *zantedeschia* lilies (p 87)

5 trailing stems of piper foliage (p 136)

2 stems of ixia, plus 3 extra flowers (p 88)

7 pink cordyline leaves (p137)

5 trailing stems of lollipop vine berries (p 102)

PREPARATION

1 Add 22-, 20- or 18-gauge white wires to any of the flowers and foliage that require extra support or length, taping them together using half- or full-width nile green floristry tape, depending on the size of the flowers.

ASSEMBLY

2 Take the large orange bird of paradise flower and position the three *zantedeschia* lilies against its stem. Tape them together with full-width nile green floristry tape. Add the two sets of extra bird of paradise petals/stamens to the left-hand side of the lilies to create more balance.

3 Next, create a very relaxed 'S'-shape to the bouquet using the trailing stems of piper foliage. Trim off any excess bulk wire as you work using wire cutters. Use fine-nose pliers to bend the stems into the required shape.

4 Use the ixia buds to continue the 'S'-shape in the design. Pull in the ixia flowers and the pink cordyline leaves to fill more space around the *zantedeschia* lilies.

5 Finally, soften the edges of the bouquet by adding the trailing lollipop vine berries. Display the bouquet in a slender black frosted glass vase.

2

Dream shrine

This design has a dream-like quality to it. A tropical and at the same time delicate pink passionflower forms the focal point of this cake, although the fantasy butterflies are fluttering for attention too! I'm addicted to making these wonderful butterflies and most of my students seem to love making them as well.

MATERIALS

20 cm (8 in) teardrop-shaped fruitcake placed on a thin cake board of same shape and size

750 g (1 lb 10 oz) white almond paste

750 g (1 lb 10 oz) pale pink sugarpaste

Teal beaded decorative braid

Clear alcohol (Cointreau or kirsch)

Broad dark purple satin ribbon

Non-toxic glue stick

Food-grade plastic posy pick

White flowerpaste

33-, 28- and 26-gauge white wires

Small, white seed-head stamens

Aubergine, bluegrass and plum petal dusts

Isopropyl alcohol

Nile green floristry tape

Myrtle satin dust

Blue or green non-toxic disco glitter

EQUIPMENT

Butterfly cutters (J)

Hibiscus petal veiner (SKGI)

Scalpel

Fine-nose pliers

Fine paintbrush

Dusting brushes

FLOWERS

Dream shrine spray (p 96)

Passionflower foliage (p 95)

PREPARATION

1 Cover the cake and cake drum as described on pages 11–12. Leave the cake to dry overnight.

2 Attach a band of teal beaded decorative braid around the base of the cake, using a small amount of sugarpaste softened with clear alcohol to hold it in place. Secure a band of broad dark purple satin ribbon to the cake drum's edge using non-toxic glue.

ASSEMBLY

3 Tape together the spray as described on page 96. Insert the posy pick into the top of the cake and slide the handle of the spray into it. Arrange the extra passionflower foliage at the back of the cake and position the third butterfly and foliage to the right-hand side of the display, resting on the cake drum.

FANTASY BUTTERFLIES

4 Use the butterfly cutters to cut out the four wing sections from white flowerpaste, leaving a thick ridge in each section. Wire each section onto 28-gauge white wires. Soften the edges and vein with the hibiscus petal veiner. Pinch each wing section from the base to the tip. Allow to firm up before painting/assembling.

5 To make the body, attach a ball of white flowerpaste to a hooked 26-gauge white wire. Add a smaller ball of flowerpaste for the head and a carrot shape for the abdomen. Divide the head into two sections using a scalpel. Insert two trimmed small, white seed-head stamens into the head to represent the antennae. A proboscis can be added too using a curled short length of 33-gauge white wire threaded through the head into the body and into the tail. This will also help support the shape and keep it together. Paint the whole piece with aubergine petal dust diluted with a little isopropyl alcohol.

6 Tape the two larger wing sections onto either side of the body using quarter-width nile green floristry tape. Add the two smaller wings slightly behind the larger ones. Dust the wings with a mixture of myrtle satin dust and bluegrass petal dust. Catch the tips with plum petal dust. Add painted spots and catch the tips with the diluted aubergine colouring and a fine paintbrush.

7 Add glitter tips to complete the fantasy theme. Apply a little non-toxic glue to the tips of the wings and antennae and then dip them into blue or green disco glitter. This glitter is non-toxic but not edible so it must only be used on items that will be lifted off the cake before it is cut!

Medinilla berries

There are about 150 species of medinilla that are native to the tropical regions of the Old World. The plant produces pretty white or pink flowers and some have large, fleshy and ornate bracts too. The berries of the plant are also attractive, ripening from white through to a pink/purple in colour. Common names for the plant include Malaysian grape and my favourite, the love plant!

MATERIALS

28- and 22-gauge white wires

White floristry tape

White flowerpaste

Fresh egg white

Plum, edelweiss, African violet and aubergine petal dusts

Edible spray varnish

EQUIPMENT

Wire cutters

Fine-nose pliers

Fine scissors

Dusting brushes

BERRIES

1 Cut several short lengths of 28-gauge white wire. Bend a small hook in the end of each one using fine-nose pliers. Tape over each wire, excluding the hook, with half-width white floristry tape. Use the sides of a pair of scissors to polish the stems.

2 Next, roll lots of small balls of well-kneaded white flowerpaste. Moisten the hooked end of the wire with fresh egg white and insert the hook into a ball. Pinch to secure it in place. The hooked wire should almost pierce through the tip of the berry. Repeat with the remaining balls.

3 Use fine scissors to create several small snips in the flowerpaste around the hooked area. Repeat with all the berries.

ASSEMBLY AND COLOURING

4 Tape the berries into sets of two and three using half-width white floristry tape and then tape these small groups onto a 22-gauge white wire to create a panicle (branched cluster) stem.

5 Dust the main stem with plum petal dust. Dust the berries with a mixture of plum, edelweiss and African violet petal dusts. Dust the snipped area of each berry with aubergine petal dust. Allow to dry and then spray with edible spray varnish.

Pink passionflower

As mentioned earlier with the red passionflower (see page 60), there are over 500 species of *Passiflora*, so I decided that I may as well include two in this book. The flower pictured here is similar but a little more complicated and time-consuming to make than the red passionflower.

MATERIALS

Vine, African violet, plum, edelweiss petal dusts

33-, 30-, 28-, 26-, 24-, 22- and 20-gauge white wires

White flowerpaste

Nile green floristry tape

Isopropyl alcohol

EQUIPMENT

Dusting brushes

Wire cutters

Fine paintbrush

Old toothbrush or stencil brush

Ruscus leaf cutters (TT)

PISTIL, STAMENS AND PLATFORM

1 These are made in exactly the same way as described for the red passionflower (see page 60). However, the colouring is a little different. Dust the pistil, ovary and the length of the stamens gently with vine petal dust. Tinge the upper surface of the pistil with African violet petal dust.

FILAMENTS

2 Cut about 70 or 80 short lengths of 33-gauge white wire. Attach a tiny ball of well-kneaded white flowerpaste to a dry wire and blend it onto the wire working the flowerpaste firmly between your finger and thumb to coat the required length (the exact length will depend on the variety you are making). Pinch off any excess flowerpaste from the end.

3 Smooth the length of the filament between your palms. Repeat to make the required number of filaments. Curl them as you make them and tape them in batches while still pliable around the base of the platform using quarter-width nile green floristry tape. This process is probably best done over a period of days rather than in one sitting.

4 Dust the tips fading towards the centre of each filament with a light mixture of plum, African violet and edelweiss petal dusts. Next, dilute some African violet petal dust with a little isopropyl alcohol and paint a ring of purple markings around the upperside and underside of the filaments. Use the same colour to add spots to the stamen filaments too, as well as an inner ring of colour to the platform area. To add tiny spots to the curled filaments, load an old toothbrush or stencil brush with colour and carefully flick fine spots onto each filament.

PETALS

5 These are made with white flowerpaste and the ruscus leaf cutters following the same instructions as for the red passionflower. Dust them with vine and edelweiss to the tips and use the African violet, plum, and edelweiss mixture from the base fading out towards the tips.

Dream shrine spray

Fantasy butterflies have been used in this pretty spray, acting almost as flowers filling space in the design. I love combining pink and this aqua/teal together on cakes. I prefer using these fantasy butterflies rather than specimen forms.

PREPARATION

1 First of all, add extra support or length to any of the flower, foliage or berry stems that need it using 24- or 22-gauge white wires and half-width nile green floristry tape. Extra wire will need to be added to the butterflies too.

ASSEMBLY

2 Tape the two trailing stems of piper foliage onto either side of the passionflower using half-width nile green floristry tape. Add passionflower tendrils too.

3 Add a few lengths of curled decorative silver paper-covered wire to help connect the various elements together and add detail and length to the spray too. Add the passionflower foliage around the focal flower to frame it.

4 Next, add the two groups of pink medinilla berries onto either side of the passionflower. Trim off any excess bulk wires using wire cutters and tape over with half-width nile green floristry tape.

5 Finally, thread and weave in the two butterflies, bending their wires so that they do not look too obvious in the display. Use fine-nose pliers to reposition any of the components to create a balanced result. Display the spray in a small ceramic dish – here I have used a aqua-coloured cup from a Japanese tea set.

2

3

4

Lollipop vine and rose

A pretty single rose forms the focal point to this stunning single-tiered birthday cake. Lollipop vine and medinilla berries surround the rose, illustrating that an attractive display can be achieved fairly easily using lots of berries and very few actual flowers.

MATERIALS

15 cm (6 in) round fruitcake placed on a thin cake board of the same size

350 g (12 oz) white almond paste

350 g (12 oz) Champagne sugarpaste

20 cm (8 in) slate-effect base

Magenta satin ribbon

Clear alcohol (Cointreau or kirsch)

Fine green satin ribbon

EQUIPMENT

Straight-edged sugarpaste smoother

Food-grade plastic posy pick

Fine-nose pliers

FLOWERS

Rose and lollipop spray (p 104)

PREPARATION

1 Cover the cake as described on pages 11–12. Quickly place the coated cake on top of the slate-effect base and use the straight-edged sugarpaste smoother to secure it, working the sugarpaste around the edge of the coating against the base to create a neat join. Leave to dry.

2 Attach a band of magenta satin ribbon around the base of the cake, using a small amount of sugarpaste softened with clear alcohol to hold it in place. Attach a band of fine green satin ribbon just above the magenta ribbon, holding it in place in the same way.

3 Assemble the rose and lollipop spray as described on page 104. Insert a food-grade posy pick into the top of the cake and then insert the handle of the spray into it. Arrange the trail of the spray attractively around the sides of the cake and use fine-nose pliers to re-arrange any of the flowers and berries that require attention.

Rose

The rose is not often thought of as an exotic flower.
Modern-day hybrid roses, however, owe their shape and
colour range to many of the Indian and Asian roses.

MATERIALS

28-, 26- and 18-gauge white wires
White, holly/ivy and pale green flowerpaste
Fresh egg white
Nile green floristry tape
Edelweiss, vine, daffodil, sunflower, moss,
foliage, forest, aubergine, plum and
ruby petal dusts
Edible spray varnish or half glaze (p 13)

EQUIPMENT

Fine-nose pliers
Non-stick rolling pin
Rose petal cutter set (TT-549, 550, 551)
Foam pad
Metal ball tool
Very large rose petal veiner (SKGI)
Plastic food bag
Smooth ceramic tool or cocktail stick
Kitchen paper ring former (p 8)
Dusting brushes
Non-stick board
Curved scissors

ROSE CONE CENTRE

1 Bend a large open hook in the end of an 18-gauge white wire using fine-nose pliers. Form a ball of well-kneaded white flowerpaste into a cone shape to measure about two-thirds the length of the smallest rose petal cutter you are planning to use. Moisten the hook with fresh egg white and insert it into the rounded base of the cone. Push the hook into most of the length of the cone. Pinch the base of the flowerpaste onto the wire to secure the two together.

FIRST AND SECOND LAYERS

2 Roll out the desired colour of flowerpaste fairly thinly. Cut out four petals using the smaller of the two rose petal cutters you are planning to use. Place the petals on the foam pad and soften the edges using the metal ball tool – work half on the edge of the petal and half on the pad using a rolling action with the tool. On larger flowers, vein each of the petals in turn using the double-sided very large rose petal veiner.

3 Place the first petal against the dried cone using a little fresh egg white to help stick it in place. Position it quite high against the cone so that you have enough of the petal to curl tightly to form a spiral effect around the cone. It is important that this cone is not visible from the overview of the finished rose. Do not worry about covering the cone near the base – there are plenty more petals to follow that will do that job. I tend to curl

the petal in from the left-hand side. Leave the right-hand edge of the petal slightly open so the next petal can be tucked underneath it.

4 Moisten the remaining three petals with fresh egg white and start the second layer by tucking a petal underneath the first petal on the cone. Stick down the edge of the first petal over the new petal. Place the next petal over the join created and then turn the rose to add the third petal. I tend to keep these petals open to start with so that I can get the positioning correct before tightening them around the cone to form a spiral shape. Leave one of the petals open slightly to take the first petal of the next layer. Some roses have slightly pinched petals – this can be done as you add each layer by pinching the top edge to create a slight point. This number of petals can be used to make small rosebuds but the cone base should be made slightly smaller so that the petals cover the whole of it.

THIRD, FOURTH AND FIFTH LAYERS

5 Roll out some more coloured flowerpaste and cut out nine petals using the same size cutter as before. Soften the edges and vein the petals as before. Cover the petals with a plastic food bag to stop them drying out. Tuck the first petal underneath the open petal from the previous layer of the rosebud and continue to add the other petals as described above, attaching them in layers of three petals at a time. It is

important to keep positioning petals over joins in the previous layer and not to line up petals directly behind each other. Gradually start to loosen the petals as you work on the fourth and fifth layers. Pinch and curl the edges slightly more as you attach the fifth layer.

HALF ROSE STAGE

6 Roll out some more coloured flowerpaste and cut out three petals using the larger cutter. Soften and vein as before. Start to hollow out the centre of each petal using the large metal ball tool or by rubbing the petal with your thumb.

7 Moisten the base of each petal with fresh egg white, creating a 'V'-shape. Attach to the rose as before, trying to place each petal over a join in the previous layer. Pinch either side of the petal at the base as you attach them so that it retains the cupped shape and allows the rose to breathe. Curl back the edges using the smooth ceramic tool, a cocktail stick or just your fingers to create more movement in the petal edges. I tend to curl either edge of the petal to create a more pointed petal shape. At this stage you have made what is termed a 'half rose'.

FULL ROSE – OUTER WIRED PETALS

8 Roll out some more flowerpaste leaving a thick ridge for the wire. Cut out the petal shape using the same size of cutter used in step 6. Hook, moisten with egg white and insert a 26-gauge white wire into the base of the ridge. Soften and vein as before. Hollow the centre of the petal with your fingers and

thumb and curl the side edges as desired. Allow to firm up in a kitchen paper ring former. Repeat to make 8–10 petals.

ASSEMBLY AND COLOURING

9 Tape the wired petals around the half rose before they have a chance to fully dry. This will enable a little reshaping. Use half width nile green floristry tape to attach the first petal over a join. Place the second petal over a join on the opposite side of the rose and then continue adding the remaing petals in the same way.

10 Mix together edelweiss, vine, daffodil and sunflower petal dusts. Probe the flower with a brush loaded with this mix to add a 'glow' at the base of each petal on the back and front. I tend to be heavier with this colour on the back of the petals. The rose pictured has been dusted lightly with a very light mixture of vine, moss and edelweiss petal dusts.

CALYX

11 Cut five lengths of 28-gauge white wire. Work a ball of holly/ivy flowerpaste onto the wire creating a long, tapered carrot shape. Place the shape against the non-stick board and flatten using the flat side of one of the double-sided veiners. If the shape looks distorted, simply trim into shape with a pair of scissors.

12 Place the flattened shape onto the foam pad and soften and hollow out the length using the metal ball tool.

Pinch the sepal from the base to the tip. Cut fine 'hairs' into the edge of the sepal using curved scissors. Repeat to make five sepals.

13 Dust each sepal on the outer surface with a mixture of foliage and forest petal dusts. Add tinges of aubergine mixed with plum or ruby petal dust. Using the same brush as for the green mixture, dust lightly on the inner surface of each sepal with edelweiss petal dust. Lightly glaze the back of each sepal with edible spray varnish or half glaze. Next, tape the five sepals to the base of the rose, positioning a sepal over a join. Add a ball of pale green flowerpaste for the ovary and pinch and squeeze it into a neat shape. Dust and glaze to match the sepals.

Lollipop vine

These ornate African berries that are also sometimes known as the marble vine (*Diplocyclos palmatus*) are actually part of the Cucurbitaceae family that includes the cucumber, marrow, squash, pumpkin, gourd, gherkin and melon.

TENDRILS

1 The tendrils are optional as they are often cut off by the florist or flower arranger prior to use. Take several lengths of 33-gauge white wire (or 35-gauge if you can get it). Use a food preparation anti-bacterial wipe or isopropyl alcohol on a piece of tissue and dip it into some vine and a touch of foliage petal dusts. Wipe the now moist colour down the length of the wires to colour them a light green. You can sometimes buy good-quality pale green 33-gauge wire, which will make things a lot easier, however, do not be tempted to use the dark green wires that are more easily available. Wrap and spiral the wires around a fine-handled paintbrush or similar to create spring-like tendrils. Spray lightly with edible spray varnish to seal the colour onto the wires.

BERRIES

2 Roll a small ball of well-kneaded very pale vine green flowerpaste. Insert a short length of 30- or 28-gauge white wire moistened with fresh egg white into the ball and then work the ball onto the wire a little, creating a more oval-shaped fruit. Push the wire a little further into the fruit so that it almost pierces through the flowerpaste. Pinch the flowerpaste around the wire to create a fine sharp point. Pinch the paste at the base of the wire to secure it.

3 Use the scalpel or plain-edge cutting wheel to lightly draw five or six lines down the sides of the fruit. Repeat to make graduating sizes of fruit.

COLOURING AND ASSEMBLY

4 Dust the unripened fruit with a mixture of vine and moss petal dusts. As the fruit ripens, start to introduce a little tangerine petal dust and then gradual coral, red and a touch of ruby for the fully ripened fruit. The odd tinge of foliage petal dust here and there can be good too.

5 Dilute some white petal dust with isopropyl alcohol and, using a fine paintbrush, add spotted lines over the lines already marked on the surface of the fruit. Try not to be too light- or heavy-handed with this.

6 Tape the berries in pairs and sets of three and four at intervals onto a length of 24-gauge white wire using half-width nile green floristry tape. Introduce an extra 24-gauge white wire as the stem progresses if you need extra length or strength to support the weight of the berries. The tendrils may also be added with each group of berries, alternating the position as you add each one. Bend and curve the main stem as you work to create an interesting shape. Glaze the berries with edible spray varnish.

MATERIALS

35- (optional), 33-, 30-, 28- and 24-gauge white wires

Anti-bacterial wipes (optional)

Isopropyl alcohol

Tissue

Vine, foliage, moss, tangerine, coral, red, ruby and white petal dusts

Edible spray varnish

Very pale vine green flowerpaste

Fresh egg white

Nile green floristry tape

EQUIPMENT

Fine paintbrush

Non-stick rolling pin

Scalpel or plain-edge cutting wheel

Dusting brushes

Fine-nose pliers

King tillandsia

Tillandsia xerographica is often known as the king of air plants. The plants are native to South America where they are found growing in Ceiba and bread trees. The silver curly form of this plant makes it an ideal component for flower arranging and bouquets too.

MATERIALS

Pale green flowerpaste

26- and 24-gauge white wires

Fresh egg white

Edelweiss, foliage, forest and aubergine petal dusts

White bridal satin dust

White floristry tape

EQUIPMENT

Non-stick rolling pin

Scalpel or plain-edge cutting wheel

Foam pad

Large metal ball tool

Stargazer B or large tulip leaf veiner (SKGI)

Dusting brushes

LEAVES

1 Roll out some well-kneaded pale green flowerpaste, leaving a thick ridge for the wire. Using a scalpel or plain-edge cutting wheel, use a freehand cutting technique to cut out a long, slender pointed leaf shape.

2 Insert a 26- or 24-gauge white wire moistened with fresh egg white into the thick ridge of the leaf to support half to three-quarters of the length of the leaf. Place the leaf onto the foam pad and use the large metal ball tool to soften the edges.

3 Texture the surface of the leaf using the double-sided stargazer B petal or large tulip leaf veiner, pressing the two sides together firmly against the flowerpaste. Remove the leaf from the veiner and pinch it from the base through to the tip, curving and curling the stem into shape to give movement and a more interesting shape. Repeat to make leaves in varying sizes.

COLOURING

4 Mix together edelweiss petal dust with a little foliage and forest to make a light-greyish green. Use the mixture to colour each leaf, dusting from the base through to the tip on both sides of each leaf. Add a tinge of aubergine to the base and the very tip edges. Over-dust each leaf with white bridal satin dust.

5 Tape the leaves into clusters using half-width white floristry tape or use the leaves individually. Hold over a jet of steam from a kettle or clothes steamer to set the colour and take away the very dry finish left by the layers of petal dust.

ALTERNATIVE METHOD FOR LEAVES

6 An alternative method to make the leaves is to work a ball of well-kneaded pale green flowerpaste onto a white wire, blending it into a finer point towards the tip of the wire. Place the leaf against a non-stick board and flatten it using the flat side of one of the veiners. Place on a foam pad and soften the edges, and then vein, pinch and curl the leaves as described above. This method often adds more variation in size and shape.

Rose and lollipop spray

The trails of lollipop vine berries are wonderful for providing not only exciting colour to this pretty spray but also a framed outline and structured shape. The berry theme is continued with contrasting pink medinilla berries, adding a cooler note of colour to this otherwise warm-coloured spray.

MATERIALS

22-gauge white wires

Nile green floristry tape

Magenta, green and gold paper-covered wires

Leaf-effect giftwrap ribbon (optional)

EQUIPMENT

Wire cutters

Small filigree silver candle holder (optional)

FLOWERS

1 full rose dusted with a mixture of plum, coral and edelweiss petal dusts (p 100)

3 anthurium flowers (p 28)

7 folded lotus leaves (p 121)

5 trails of lollipop vine berries (p 102)

2 groups of silver tillandsia leaves (p 103)

3 groups of medinilla berries (p 94)

PREPARATION

1 Tape any of the flowers and foliage that need extra support onto 22-gauge white wires using half-width nile green floristry tape.

ASSEMBLY

2 Surround the rose with the three anthurium flowers and tape together with half-width nile green floristry tape. Fill in the gaps by positioning the folded lotus leaves in between the anthuriums, slightly recessed in the spray. Trim off any excess bulk wire using wire cutters.

3 Next add the trails of lollipop vine berries using a couple of lengths looped behind the rose at the top of the spray and the others creating a long trail to the tip. Pull and tape in a couple of groups of tillandsia leaves opposite each other around the rose.

4 Next, add loops and trails of magenta, green and gold paper-covered wires to continue the framework provided by the lollipop vine berries. Curl the very ends of the wires at the tip of the long trail.

5 Add the three groups of medinilla berries evenly spaced around the spray for extra colour and to fill in the remaining gaps. Finally, weave and trail a couple of lengths of leaf-effect giftwrap ribbon around the trails of berries and paper-covered wires. Display the spray in a small filigree silver candle holder.

Orchid vine wedding

Vanilla orchids, vanilla pods, pink passionflowers with their fruit and trailing vines add an interesting tropical element to the more traditionally favoured bridal rose. A painted coloured cocoa butter design of a vanilla orchid and its foliage completes this romantic two-tiered wedding cake.

MATERIALS

15 cm (6 in) teardrop-shaped polystyrene dummy cake

25 cm (10 in) teardrop rich fruitcake placed on a thin cake board of the same size

1 kg (2 lb 3 oz) white almond paste

1.4 kg (3 lb 2 oz) white sugarpaste

Pale lilac satin ribbon

Clear alcohol (Cointreau or kirsch)

Cocoa butter, grated

Mug and saucer

Edelweiss, vine, white, foliage, African violet and sunflower petal dusts

Food-grade plastic posy pick (optional)

EQUIPMENT

Tracing paper and pencil

Fine scriber or pen that has run dry

Fine paintbrushes

Large corsage pins (or grippy mat or double-sided strong carpet tape)

Tall Perspex tilting cake stand (CC)

Fine-nose pliers

FLOWERS

Orchid vine bouquet (p 114)

Four trails of piper foliage (p 136)

1 It is much safer using a lighter polystyrene dummy cake for the top tier of the display as the cake is placed on a tilting cake stand and could potentially slide off. A real cake could be used but I always prefer to use a dummy cake instead and provide an extra cutting cake if needed. Cover both the dummy cake and fruitcake as described on pages 11–12, but leave off the white almond paste covering on the dummy cake. Leave to dry for several days. Attach a band of pale lilac satin ribbon around the base of each cake, using a small amount of sugarpaste softened with clear alcohol to hold the ribbon in place.

COCOA PAINTING

2 Paint this design freehand onto the cake or use the template on page 142. Trace the vanilla orchid design onto a sheet of tracing paper. Use a fine scriber to scribe the design onto the surface of the larger cake. Melt a small amount of grated cocoa butter onto a saucer above a mug of boiled water.

3 Add coloured petal dusts as required into the melted cocoa butter to create a painting medium to execute the design using fine paintbrushes. The addition of a touch of edelweiss petal dust makes the finish more opaque. Use vine and white petal dusts to paint the outer petals of the vanilla orchid. Allow the first painted layer to dry before adding extra depth or detail. Add a touch more vine to the mixture to paint depth, and then add a touch of foliage to add an outline and fine veins on the petals. Mix up another small amount of melted cocoa butter with white and African violet petal dusts to paint the orchid lip. Again, once this layer has set, increase the depth of colour with more African violet to add extra detail. Use a small amount of sunflower and white to colour the very heart of the lip petal. The leaves too are painted in layers using vine, foliage and a touch of white. Allow to dry.

ASSEMBLY

4 There are holes on the slanted section of the tilting stand. Place the coated dummy cake on top of the slant and carefully insert large corsage pins up through the stand and into the polystyrene to hold the cake in place. If you are using a real cake, then a piece of grippy mat or double-sided strong carpet tape works well. Otherwise the stand is supplied with perspex pins that can be inserted through a cake board and up into a real cake. However, this means you will need to drill holes in the cake board in the appropriate places prior to coating the cake. Use a shorter tilting stand to display the base tier. Insert the handle of the tropical vine bouquet directly into the dummy cake (for a real cake you would need to use a food-grade plastic posy pick pushed into the cake to hold the bouquet). Use fine-nose pliers to rearrange any of the flowers and foliage that need it. Carefully trail the length of the bouquet around the top tier and over the side of the base tier. Use the trailing stems of piper foliage to help frame the display, tucking the stems underneath the cakes.

Vanilla orchid

There are over a hundred species of vanilla orchid, although there are only a few grown commercially that are used to produce culinary vanilla pods. Seventy-five percent of all commercial vanilla is grown in Madagascar, Comores and the Reunion Islands. The rest is produced in Indonesia, Tonga, Tahiti and Mexico. The flowers can be white, creamy white, creamy green and yellow, often with a stronger yellow lip. The variety illustrated here, *Vanilla imperialis*, has a purple and sometimes pink colouring to the lip petal, making it an eye-catching flower.

COLUMN

1 Roll a small ball of well-kneaded white flowerpaste. Insert a 24-gauge white wire into the ball and work the flowerpaste down the wire to create quite a slender column. Try to keep the tip of the column slightly broader than the base. Place the length of the column against the length of the rounded end of the ceramic silk veining tool. Press the column against the tool to hollow out the underside using your finger and thumb, which will in turn create a subtle ridge down the upper side of the column.

Remove from the tool and bend the length carefully into a lazy 'S'-shape. Add a tiny ball of white flowerpaste to the tip of the column to represent the anther cap. Use a scalpel to mark a line down the centre of the anther cap. Leave to dry for several hours.

LIP (LABELLUM)

2 Roll out some well-kneaded white flowerpaste, leaving a thick ridge down the centre. Use the lip cutter from the vanilla orchid set or refer to the template on page 142 and use a scalpel to cut out the lip shape. Use the metal ball tool to soften the edge of the petal and then place it into the double-sided wide amaryllis petal veiner.

3 Place the petal back onto the non-stick board and use the broad end of the dresden tool to double-frill the edge by pressing and pulling the flowerpaste against the board at close intervals to create a slightly ragged, frilled edge.

4 Use the ceramic silk veining tool to frill over the top of the ragged frills to create a more softened frilled edge. Place the petal onto the foam pad or onto your

MATERIALS

White, pale green and mid-green flowerpaste
28-, 26-, 24-, 22- and 18-gauge white wires
Fresh egg white
African violet, daffodil, sunflower, edelweiss, vine, foliage, aubergine and forest petal dusts
Isopropyl alcohol
Nile green and white (optional) floristry tape
Edible spray varnish

Medium and large metal ball tools
Wide amaryllis petal veiner (SKGI)
Non-stick board
Dresden tool
Foam pad
Dusting brushes
Fine and very fine paintbrushes
Stargazer B petal veiner
Plain-edge cutting wheel
Grooved board (optional)
Large tulip leaf veiner (SKGI)
Scissors

EQUIPMENT

Non-stick rolling pin
Ceramic silk veining tool
Scalpel
Vanilla orchid cutter set (TT827–830)

palm and hollow out either side of the thick ridge using the medium metal ball tool.

5 Moisten the side edges of the petal shape with fresh egg white. Place the column, hollowed-side down towards the petal, and carefully attach the two side edges onto the sides of the column. Pinch in place to secure the two together, leaving a little of the 'backbone' of the column on show. Curl back the frilled edges of the petal using your fingers and thumb. Open up the throat if needed using the broad end of the dresden tool to create a gap between the column and the lip/labellum. Allow to dry before colouring.

COLOURING

6 Dust the frilled edges of the lip/labellum with African violet petal dust, working from the edges towards the centre of the lip. Leave the very heart of the petal free from the purple colouring. Use a finer brush to add a mixture of daffodil and sunflower petal dusts at the heart of the petal.

7 Next dilute some African violet petal dust with isopropyl alcohol and paint some fine lines radiating from the yellow section of the lip fading out towards the edges using a very fine paintbrush.

SIDE/WING/ARMS (LATERAL) PETALS

8 Roll out some well-kneaded white flowerpaste, leaving a thick ridge for the wire. Cut out a lateral petal using the smaller finer curved cutter in the vanilla orchid cutter set or use a scalpel to cut out the template on page 142. Moisten the end of a third of a length of 28-gauge white wire with water and insert it into the thick ridge of the petal so that it supports about a third to half the length of the petal.

9 Place the petal on your palm or on the foam pad and soften the edge working half on the flowerpaste and half on your palm/pad. Do not frill the edges: you are simply trying to take away the harsh cut edge.

10 Place the petal into the double-sided stargazer B petal veiner and press firmly to texture the surface. Remove the petal from the veiner and gently pinch it from the base through to the tip, curving the petal a little as you handle it. Repeat the process, turning the cutter over to create a mirror image of the first petal.

HEAD (DORSAL SEPAL)

11 Roll out some more well-kneaded white flowerpaste, leaving a thick ridge for the wire. Use the straightest cutter from the vanilla orchid cutter set or use the template on page 142 and a scalpel to cut out the dorsal sepal. Insert 28-gauge white wire moistened with fresh egg white to support about half the length of the petal. Soften the edges as before and texture using the stargazer B petal veiner. Pinch the petal from the base to the tip to accentuate the central vein and curve it as if trying to create a fully matured flower or leaf — fairly straight with a slight curve at the tip for a just-opened flower finish.

LEGS (LATERAL SEPALS)

12 These are made in the same way as the dorsal sepal but using the remaining broader, slightly curved cutter or the lateral sepal template on page 142. Once again, you will need to turn the cutter over to create a left and right sepal. Pinch each sepal from the base to accentuate the

central vein and create a slightly curved shape at the same time.

COLOURING AND ASSEMBLY

13 Mix together edelweiss and vine petal dusts. Dust each petal and sepal from the base, fading out slightly towards the edges using a flat dusting brush. Then bring in a little of the same colour, dusting from the edges towards the centre of each petal/sepal.

14 Tape the lateral sepals onto either side of the lip/labellum using half-width nile green floristry tape. It helps at this stage if the petals are not quite dry and are still pliable so that a little reshaping can be achieved easily to create a more natural shape. Next, tape the dorsal sepal positioned just behind the two lateral petals and then finally add the two lateral petals at the base of the flower. Reshape the petals and sepals as desired.

OVARY

15 This is the part of the orchid that develops into the vanilla pod. Add a sausage of pale green flowerpaste onto the main stem. Thin it between your fingers and thumb to create a slender ovary shape. Trim away any excess using the scalpel. Curve the ovary/stem gently. Use the plain-edge cutting wheel to mark a few gentle veins down the length of the ovary. Dust lightly with vine and foliage petal dusts. Tinge the base and just behind the sepals/petals with a touch of aubergine petal dust.

16 Allow the petals to dry and then use a jet of steam from a just-boiled kettle or a clothes steamer to set the colour and take away the dry just-dusted appearance.

BUDS

17 Form a ball of well-kneaded white flowerpaste into a cone shape. Bend a hook in the end of a 24-gauge white wire. Moisten the hook with water and insert it into the broad end of the cone. Work the base of the cone between your finger and thumb to create an elongated slender neck. Use the plain-edge cutting wheel to divide the surface into three, to represent the three outer sepals. Create a series of fine lines using either the scalpel or the plain-edge cutting wheel. Bend the neck of the bud gently. Add an ovary as for the flower but keeping it much finer and shorter. Dust the bud with the same vine/edelweiss mixture used on the outer petals/sepals. Dust the ovary as for the flower too.

VANILLA PODS

18 I have made these in their early green stage when they are fleshier than the more familiar dried, wizened appearance. Form a long, fine, bean shape using mid-green flowerpaste. Insert a hooked 24- or 22-gauge white wire into the bean and pinch the flowerpaste firmly around the wire. The gauge of wire will depend on the size of the bean/pod you are making. Smooth the flowerpaste between your palms.

19 Use the plain-edge cutting wheel to mark a central vein down the length of the pod. Curve it gracefully. Some vanilla plants produce very straight pods, while others produce more curved, fine, banana-like pods. Repeat to make the required number of pods. Allow them to firm up a little before dusting.

20 Dust the pods lightly with forest petal dust. Over-dust with a mixture of edelweiss and foliage petal dusts.

Catch the tip and base of the pod with aubergine. Tape into groups of two, three or more using half-width nile green floristry tape. Spray lightly with edible spray varnish.

LEAVES

21 The leaves are very fleshy and thick in form. I usually make them much finer than the real thing. Roll out some mid-green flowerpaste, leaving a thick ridge – you could use a grooved board for this purpose. Cut out the leaf shape using the plain-edge cutting wheel. Insert a 28-, 26- or 24-gauge white wire moistened with fresh egg white into the central ridge to support about half its length. The gauge of wire will depend on the size of the leaf you are making.

22 Soften the edge of the leaf with the large metal ball tool and then vein using either the double-sided stargazer B petal veiner or the large tulip leaf veiner. Remove the leaf from the veiner and pinch it from the base to the tip to accentuate the central vein. Repeat to make numerous leaves in varying sizes. Allow them to dry a little before dusting.

23 Dust the leaves in layers with forest, foliage and vine petal dusts. Allow to dry and then spray with edible spray varnish The leaves are quite glossy so you might need to spray the leaves a couple of times to give them a good coating of glaze.

AERIAL ROOTS

24 These are optional. They grow out of the leaf axils at intervals down the stem. To make them, tape over short lengths of 28-gauge white wire with half-width white floristry tape. Tape over each a few times but each time start taping lower from the tip to create a fine tapered effect. Smooth over the tape to blend the joins using the side of a pair of scissors. Dust the tips with vine petal dust.

FINAL ASSEMBLY

25 Tape an aerial root onto the end of an 18-gauge white wire using half-width nile green floristry tape. Add a small leaf at the same join and then continue to add the leaves down the stem, alternating their position as you add them. Thicken the stem with full-width nile green floristry tape as you work down onto the larger leaves. Gradually introduce small groups of buds, adding a leaf where they join the main stem, then add the flowers and more buds in clusters too. Dust the main stem with foliage and vine petal dusts. Spray with edible spray varnish to give shiny stems. Other trailing stems of foliage can be formed to add the groups of vanilla pods.

Begonia

There are lots of species of begonia widely distributed throughout the tropics and subtropics, but particularly in South America. I love creating and using these highly decorative leaves as they add an instant touch of the exotic to any arrangement or cake display.

MATERIALS

Pale green flowerpaste
24-, 22- and 20-gauge white wires
Cornflour
Plum, aubergine and foliage petal dusts
Isopropyl alcohol
Myrtle bridal satin dust
Edible spray varnish

EQUIPMENT

Non-stick rolling pin
Plain-edge cutting wheel
Dusting brushes
Begonia leaf veiner (SKGI)
Non-stick board
Dresden tool
Dimpled foam
Fine paintbrush

LEAVES

1 Roll out some well-kneaded pale green flowerpaste fairly thickly, leaving a thicker ridge at the centre to hold the wire. The veiners have quite deep veins and so it is important not to roll the flowerpaste too thinly. Trim away excess flowerpaste using the plain-edge cutting wheel and then insert a 24-, 22- or 20-gauge white wire moistened with fresh egg white into the ridge. The exact gauge will depend on the size of the leaf you are making.

2 Dust the double-sided begonia leaf veiner very lightly with cornflour and position the wired flowerpaste into the back half of the veiner so that the ridge is against it. Try to line up the wire with the central veiner of the leaf. Carefully position the top half of the veiner on top and press firmly to texture the leaf. Remove the leaf from the veiner and place it against the non-stick board. Next, use the plain-edge cutting wheel to trim around the edge of the leaf.

3 Turn the leaf over so that the upper surface is against the non-stick board and then create a jagged edge using the broad side of the dresden tool, pulling and dragging the tool against the flowerpaste onto the non-stick board at intervals. Pinch the leaf from behind through to the tip to

shape it and accentuate the central vein. Place the leaf onto dimpled foam to support it as it dries. Repeat to make the required number of leaves. Tape over each leaf stem a few times with half-width nile green floristry tape.

COLOURING

4 Dust a splash of plum petal dust onto the upper surface of the leaf from the area where the wire comes out to taper down the central vein slightly. Dust the back of the leaf with plum petal dust and over-dust with aubergine. Next, use foliage petal dust on the edge of the upper surface, bringing the colour into the main body of the leaf.

5 Dilute some aubergine petal dust with isopropyl alcohol and paint in some of the fine veins radiating from the base of the leaf using a fine paintbrush. Add a border of this diluted colour around the very jagged edge of the leaf too.

6 Dilute some myrtle bridal satin dust with isopropyl alcohol and add dotted highlights around the leaf in between the veins. Allow to dry and then spray lightly with edible spray varnish.

Senecio

I came across this succulent recently in a garden centre – its name struck me as fun – *Senecio* 'Kilimanjaro'. However, its size and simplicity to make also appealed to me. Succulents are wonderful to make, being fairly quick and providing a bulk that fills an arrangement quickly and effectively.

MATERIALS

30-, 28- and 26-gauge white wires
Pale green flowerpaste
Fresh egg white
Nile green floristry tape
Forest, foliage, white, edelweiss and aubergine petal dusts
Edible spray varnish

EQUIPMENT

Wire cutters
Plain-edge cutting wheel
Dusting brushes
Fine-nose pliers

LEAVES

1 Cut several short lengths of 30-, 28- or 26-gauge white wires, depending on the size of leaves you are making. Next, take a piece of well-kneaded pale green flowerpaste and form it into a ball. Insert a wire moistened with fresh egg white into the ball and then carefully work the flowerpaste down the wire to create the length of the leaf. Smooth the leaf between your palms.

2 Use the plain-edge cutting wheel to mark a single line down the leaf to represent the central vein. Repeat to make leaves in varying sizes.

ASSEMBLY

3 The leaves may be dusted before assembly – I prefer to assemble and then colour them as they are easier to handle this way. Use a 26-gauge white wire as a leader wire to start taping a few smaller leaves around the end using half-width nile green floristry tape. Continue adding leaves around the wire, gradually increasing in size as you work. If the leaves are still pliable this will allow you to reshape them a little to give a more realistic effect.

COLOURING

4 Mix together forest, foliage and white (edelweiss in mats) petal dusts. Use a large dusting brush to apply colour all over the leaves and the main stem. Add tinges of aubergine petal dust here and there if desired to help break up the space. Allow to dry and then spray lightly with edible spray varnish.

Orchid vine bouquet

Although the rose is essentially the focal flower of this unusual bouquet, it is the tropical vanilla orchids and pink passionflower that provide the real interest. I love combining unusual exotic and tropical flowers and foliage with more familiar floral elements.

MATERIALS

22-, 20- and 18-gauge white wires

Nile green floristry tape

Green florist's twine

EQUIPMENT

Wire cutters

Fine-nose pliers

Tall frosted glass vase

FLOWER AND FOLIAGE

2 full roses, coloured with a mixture of plum, African violet, white and aubergine petal dusts (p 100)

3 trails of vanilla foliage, 3 vanilla orchids and 3 vanilla pods (p 108)

1 pink passionflower, 3 trails of foliage and 3 fruit (p 95)

3 begonia leaves (p 112)

3 small groups of senecio foliage (p 113)

5 Joseph's coat leaves (p 38)

3 ladder fern leaves (p 55)

PREPARATION

1 Add length and strength to any of the flower and foliage stems that require it by taping them on to 22-, 20- or 18-gauge white wires using half-width nile green floristry tape.

ASSEMBLY

2 Use the green florist's twine to create a tangled ball with a single trail to create the length of the bouquet. Pull the end of the twine at the centre of the tangled ball to create a handle for the bouquet. Next, tape in the two full pink roses to fill the focal area of the bouquet using half-width nile green floristry tape and bind them to the twine handle.

3 Use the lengths of vanilla foliage to trail from the centre of the bouquet to the tip. Add more vanilla foliage to fill the edge of the upper area of the bouquet. Tape the three vanilla orchids around the roses so that they are evenly spaced. Next, add the vanilla pods to hang at the base of the bouquet and the pink passionflower next to the bottom vanilla orchid. Trim off any excess wires as you work using wire cutters.

4 Fill in around the bouquet with the passionflower trailing foliage and its fruit, then add the begonia and senecio leaves to create interest around the roses.

5 Finally add the Joseph's coat foliage and fern leaves to add further interest and fill in the remaining gaps in the bouquet. Tape over the handle of the bouquet with full-width nile green floristry tape to neaten. Use fine-nose pliers to adjust and curve any of the flower and foliage stems that might need relaxing a little. Display in a tall frosted glass vase.

2

3

4

Indian dream

The clashing colours of the sacred pink lotus and the spidery ylang-ylang flowers form a stunning display on this single-tiered cake. Curls of pink, green and yellow decorative paper-covered wires help to connect and blend the flowers and foliage together.

MATERIALS

25 cm (10 in) round rich fruitcake placed on a thin cake board of the same size

1.25 kg (2 lb 12 oz) white almond paste

1.25 kg (2 lb 12 oz) white sugarpaste

36 cm (14 in) round cake drum

Fine yellow and green decorative braid

Clear alcohol (Cointreau or kirsch)

Broad green satin ribbon

Non-toxic glue stick

Nile green floristry tape

Pink, yellow and green decorative paper-covered wires

Food-grade plastic posy pick

EQUIPMENT

Straight-edged sugarpaste smoother

Fine-nose pliers

FLOWERS

8 ylang-ylang flowers, plus foliage (p 22)

1 sacred lotus, plus folded leaves (p 118)

5 groups of ylang-ylang berries (p 23)

3 trailing stems of decorative Chinese yam (p 21)

PREPARATION

1 Cover the cake and cake drum as described on pages 11–12. Place the cake onto the drum and use the straight-edged sugarpaste smoother to blend the join between the cake and the board. Leave to dry overnight.

2 Attach a band of fine yellow and green braid around the base of the cake, using a small amount of sugarpaste softened with clear alcohol to hold it in place. Secure a band of broad green satin ribbon to the cake drum's edge using non-toxic glue.

SPRAY

3 Tape the ylang-ylang flowers and foliage onto either side of the sacred lotus flower using half-width nile green floristry tape. Next surround and fill the space around the lotus with the folded lotus leaves and start to introduce the ylang-ylang berries too.

4 Create more of an 'S'-shape to the display using the trailing stems of yam leaves. Curve the stems using fine-nose pliers. To complete the spray, add curled lengths of pink, yellow and green decorative paper-covered wires to add more interest and to define the shape of the spray. Use some of the wires to weave through the flowers around the focal area too.

5 Insert a food-grade plastic posy pick into the top of the cake and slide the handle of the spray into it. Use fine-nose pliers to bend any of the flowers and foliage that require repositioning.

Sacred lotus

There several forms of lotus (*Nelumbo*), with the flower varying in size and form, although the colour is always in varying shades of pink or white, or in the case of the American lotus, yellow. The lotus is the national flower of India where it is linked with mythology and prayer. The dried seed-heads of the flower are used as decorations and in flower arranging. The dried stamens are used in China to make a fragrant herbal tea and food is often served on the leaves. Even the seeds are edible, eaten raw or dried and cooked like popcorn, or they can be boiled and turned into a paste with sugar and used in pastries, such as mooncakes or as a flavouring for rice pudding. The roots are also sliced and pickled or can be cooked into crisp decorative chips.

POD/OVARY

1 I find it easier to make this section of the flower with cold porcelain so that I can use non-toxic glue to bond the stamens around the pod. Bend a large hook in the end of an 18-gauge white wire using fine-nose pliers. Roll a ball of pale green cold porcelain and then form it into a cone shape. Moisten the hooked wire with water and insert it into the fine end of the cone.

2 Work the cold porcelain down onto the wire to elongate the cone slightly. Next, flatten the top of the shape and pinch around the sides to create a sharper edge.

3 Use fine plain-edged angled tweezers to pinch a slight ridge around the circumference of the shape. Next, use the pointed end of the smooth ceramic tool to create several indents in the upper surface of the pod.

4 Roll lots of tiny balls of pale green cold porcelain and drop one into each of the holes on the pod. Use the needle tool or a strong wire to indent the centre of each of the balls.

EQUIPMENT

Fine-nose pliers
Fine plain-edged angled tweezers
Smooth ceramic tool
Needle tool or strong wire
Dusting brushes
Large scissors
Non-stick rolling pin
Large cymbidium orchid cutter (TT) or use the lotus petal template on p 140
Plain-edge cutting wheel
Foam pad
Large metal ball tool
Wide amaryllis petal veiner (SKGI)
Kitchen paper ring former (p 8)
Sage leaf cutters (TT852, 855) or use the lotus petal template on p 140
Wide diamond jubilee rose petal cutters (TT776, 777)
Very large nasturtium leaf veiner (SKGI)

MATERIALS

26-, 24-, 22-, 20- and 18- gauge white wires
Pale green cold porcelain
Vine, foliage, aubergine, sunflower, edelweiss, plum, African violet and forest petal dusts
White seed-head stamens
Non-toxic craft glue
White and mid-green flowerpaste
Fresh egg white
Nile green floristry tape
Edible spray varnish

5 Dust the pod as desired. The colour varies between varieties – it can be creamy, yellow, bright green or a darker, almost blue-green colour with aubergine tinges too. Here I have used vine and foliage green and then tinged gently with aubergine petal dust.

STAMENS

6 You will need one-and-a-half to two bunches of white seed-head stamens for each flower. Divide the stamens into several smaller groups and line up their tips. Bond each group together with a little non-toxic craft glue at the centre. Squeeze the glue with your finger and thumb to create a neat line of glue at the centre. Flatten the stamens as you work. Allow the glue to set and then cut the stamens in half using a large pair of scissors.

7 Trim the stamens a little shorter if needed – you will be able to tell if you try one group against the pod to see if they are going to be too long. Apply a little more non-toxic craft glue to each group in turn and add them around the pod. Hold each group firmly against the pod to the count of ten. This should allow the glue to become tacky and hold the stamens in place. Try not to use too much glue as this

will take too long to dry and result in the stamens dropping off. Once you have created a nice full stamen centre leave it to dry before colouring.

8 Use the tweezers to pull and curl the stamens out a little, creating a more realistic effect. Use sunflower petal dust to colour the anther tips of the stamens. Use vine petal dust on the filament lengths of the stamens.

PETALS

9 The number and size of petals varies on each flower. Start with the largest petals as these will take the longest to dry. Roll out some well-kneaded white flowerpaste, leaving a thick ridge for the wire. Use the large cymbidium orchid cutter to cut out the petal shape or refer to the template on page 140 and use the plain-edge cutting wheel to cut out the shape.

10 Insert a 24-gauge white wire moistened with fresh egg white into the thick ridge to support about a third to half the length of the petal. Pinch the flowerpaste slightly at the base down onto the wire to elongate it.

11 Place the petal on your palm or the foam pad and soften the edges using the large metal ball tool and a rolling action to take away the cut edge. Try not to frill the edges.

12 Place the petal into the double-sided wide amaryllis petal veiner and press the two sides together to texture the petal. Remove the petal from the veiner and hollow out the length of the petal using the large metal ball tool or your fingers and thumb.

13 Rest the petal in a kitchen paper ring former until it is a little firmer and holding its shape well. Repeat to make several wired petals in varying sizes, using the sage leaf cutters for the smaller petals.

COLOURING AND ASSEMBLY

14 Dust the base of each of the petals with a light mixture of vine and edelweiss petal dusts. Next, mix together plum petal dust with a touch of African violet and dust the petals from the edges, fading towards the base on both sides of each petal.

15 Tape the petals around the stamen centre using half-width nile green floristry tape, starting with the smaller petals and then increasing the size using the largest petals last. Use the side of a pair of scissors to polish the stem and disguise the lines created by the floristry tape. If the petals are still pliable as you assemble the flower, then this will enable you to reshape them, giving a more realistic finish. Allow to dry and then hold the flower over a jet of steam from a kettle or clothes steamer – this will set the colour to give a more waxy finish to the flower.

BUDS

16 Roll a large ball of well-kneaded white flowerpaste. Form the ball into a coin shape and then insert a hooked wire moistened with fresh egg white into the broad end of the bud. Neaten the join between the bud and the wire using your finger and thumb to blend the flowerpaste.

17 Use the plain-edge cutting wheel to divide the length of the bud into three sections. Roll out some more white flowerpaste and cut out six petal shapes using the smallest sage cutter or the template on page 140. Soften the edges and vein as for the wired petals.

18 Attach the petals onto the sides of the bud using fresh egg white. Pinch the base and the tips as you add each one to create a more pointed finish. To create larger buds, add some extra wired petals. Colour the bud in the same way as the flower.

LEAVES

19 The leaves of the lotus are rather large and round in shape, making them often quite difficult to make and use on cakes. I find it easier to treat the leaves as a florist would often use them: folded and curled, creating a more interesting shape behind the flower. Roll out some mid-green flowerpaste, leaving a thick ridge for the wire. These leaves are quite large and fleshy. Cut out the leaf using one of the wide diamond jubilee rose petal cutters.

20 Insert a 22- or 20-gauge white wire moistened with fresh egg white into the thick ridge to support about half the length of the leaf. Place the leaf onto the foam pad and soften the edges using the large metal ball tool.

21 Next, vein the leaf using the double-sided very large nasturtium leaf veiner. Press the two sides together firmly to create a strong vein. Remove the leaf from the veiner and carefully create folds in the leaf or roll and curl the edges as desired. Repeat to make numerous leaves that can then be taped together with half-width nile green floristry tape to create a circle shape.

COLOURING

22 Very gently dust the leaf in layers from the base to the edges with forest petal dust as this is quite a blue green. Over-dust heavily with foliage and then add a little vine on top. Use aubergine petal dust to catch the edges here and there. Allow to dry and then spray lightly with edible spray varnish.

Sacred lotus arrangement

This is an alternative display using the flowers and foliage from the Indian dream (see page 116). Once again, the props cupboard at Sue Atkinson's studio was a godsend! This green glass plate reminded me very much of the lotus leaf, making it a perfect base for this eye-catching design.

(see page 116)

MATERIALS AND EQUIPMENT

22- and 20-gauge white wires

Nile green floristry tape

Florist's staysoft or plasticine

Green glass plate (or similar)

Wire cutters

Fine-nose pliers

FLOWERS

1 sacred lotus, plus 1 bud and leaves (p 118)

8 ylang-ylang flowers, plus foliage (p 22)

3 trailing stems of decorative Chinese yam (p 21)

7 groups of ylang-ylang berries (p 23)

PREPARATION

1 First of all add extra 22- or 20-gauge white wires taped onto any of the flowers and foliage that require extra length or support using half-width nile green floristry tape. Next attach a ball of florist's staysoft onto the green glass plate. The two should simply bind together without the need for glue.

ASSEMBLY

2 Bend a hook in the end of the lotus flower stem using fine-nose pliers. This will give the flower a little more support. Insert the stem into the staysoft or plasticine, creating the focal area of the arrangement. Next, add the lotus bud to the left-hand side of the lotus, again hooking the wire. Use the ylang-ylang flowers and foliage to create a diagonal line of colour on either side of the lotus.

3 Surround the lotus with the folded lotus leaves, which will at the same time fill in the large gaps in the arrangement.

4 Add the trailing stems of yam leaves to define a more elegantly shaped display – an almost reversed, lazy 'S'-shape. Complete the arrangement by adding the groups of ylang-ylang berries, which are dotted throughout the arrangement.

Pink perfection

Two beautifully exotic looking fringed peonies adorn this elegant two-tier wedding cake. The medinilla berries have been sprayed a teal green using an edible food spray to match the ribbons used to decorate the cakes.

MATERIALS

15 cm (6 in) and 23 cm (9 in) round
fruitcakes placed on thin cake boards
of the same size

1.4 kg (3 lb 2oz) white almond paste

1.8 kg (4 lb) pink sugarpaste

33 cm (13 in) round cake drum

Narrow teal satin ribbon

Clear alcohol (Cointreau or kirsch)

Broad teal satin ribbon

Non-toxic glue stick

Nile green floristry tape

EQUIPMENT

Straight-edged sugarpaste smoother

2 food-grade plastic posy picks

Fine-nose pliers

FLOWERS

2 Pink perfection sprays (p 130)

PREPARATION

1 Cover the cakes and cake drum as described on pages 11–12. Place the small cake on top of the large cake and blend the join between them using the straight-edged sugarpaste smoother. Allow to dry overnight.

2 Attach a band of narrow teal satin ribbon around the base of both cakes using a little sugarpaste softened with clear alcohol to hold it in place at the back. Secure the broad teal satin ribbon to the cake drum's edge using non-toxic glue.

ASSEMBLY

3 Insert the two food-grade posy picks into the cakes ready to hold the sprays of flowers. Assemble and tape together the fringed peony sprays as instructed on page 130. Insert the handles of the sprays into the posy picks. Use fine-nose pliers to reposition and adjust any of the flowers, berries and foliage that require it.

Peony

I love using peonies on my cakes. They are such large showy flowers and not many are required to fill space and create instant impact. The peony illustrated here is based on a flower I bought from my local florist, which was almost but not quite the variety 'bowl of beauty'. I loved its creamy-white fringed petals at the centre of the flower. This section is fairly time-consuming to make, however, it could be made gradually over a period of days, adding the petals a few at a time. The peony originates from China where it has been cultivated for over one thousand years.

MATERIALS

Pale green, white, pale pink, and mid-green flowerpaste

33-, 30-, 28-, 26-, 24- and 22-gauge white wires

Nile green floristry tape

Vine, plum, sunflower, daffodil, edelweiss, African violet, foliage, aubergine and forest petal dusts

Fresh egg white

Edible spray varnish

EQUIPMENT

Non-stick rolling pin

Fine-nose pliers

Dusting brushes

Non-stick board

Single peony leaf veiner (SKGI)

Scissors and fine scissors

Large metal ball tool

Ceramic silk veining tool

Dresden tool

Golden jubilee rose cutters (TT)

Kitchen paper ring former (p 8)

Standard rose petal cutters (TT278-280) or use the peony petal template on p 142

Grooved board

Plain-edge cutting wheel

Cattleya orchid wing petal cutters (TT)

OVARY

1 This part of the flower can have two, three, four or sometimes more sections to it. I prefer three or four in my interpretation of the flower. Roll a small ball of well-kneaded pale green flowerpaste. Form the ball into a fine cone shape. Bend a hook in the end of a 28-gauge white wire using fine-nose pliers. Moisten the hook with water and insert it into the base of the cone, pushing it deep into the shape to give a good support. Thin the tip of the cone into a very fine point.

2 Next, pinch a gentle ridge down one side of the shape using your finger and thumb. Curl the fine tip over onto the ridged side. Repeat to make three or four equal-sized sections.

3 Tape the sections together while they are still pliable so that they sit closely together using quarter-width nile green floristry tape. Allow to dry.

4 Dust the ovary lightly with vine petal dust. Tinge the tips with plum.

FRINGED PETALS

5 These are made using a freehand technique to give more of a random formation, which is required for this style of flower. Cut several lengths of 33-gauge white wire into quarters. Insert a dry wire into a small ball of white flowerpaste and work the paste down the wire to create an elongated carrot shape with the tip being left slightly broader.

6 Place the shape onto the non-stick board and flatten it using the flat side of a leaf/petal veiner. Remove the shape from the board, trim it with scissors if the shape is too distorted and then soften the edges using the large metal ball tool.

7 Place the shape back onto the non-stick board and texture the surface using the ceramic silk veining tool to roll gently over both sides. Try not to apply too much pressure as this will make the petals too wide. Next, use the broad end of the dresden tool to flatten and pull out the edge at the very tip of the petal. This will create a tight frilled effect as well as thinning the flowerpaste, making it easier to create the fringed effect.

8 Use the fine end of the dresden tool to cut into the thinned section to create the fringe, or alternatively, use a pair of fine scissors to cut slender 'V'-shapes into the edge.

9 Pinch the petal from the base to the tip to create movement and a gentle central vein. Repeat to make a large quantity of petals – about 40 to 50. Remember, these can be built up gradually. I usually tape groups of these petals around the ovary as I am working so that I can assess just how many more petals I am going to need to complete this section. Reshape the petals as you work too.

10 Dust the petals from the base using a mixture of sunflower, daffodil and edelweiss petal dusts. Fade the colour towards the mid section. Tinge the tips of the petal very gently with plum petal dust – this is optional and will depend on the variety you are copying.

OUTER PETALS

11 Squash the golden jubilee rose cutter to create a longer slender petal shape. Roll out some well-kneaded pale pink flowerpaste, leaving a thick ridge for the wire. Cut out a petal shape using the squashed cutter or refer to the peony petal template on page 142. Insert a hooked wire moistened with fresh egg white into the thick ridge to support about a third of the petal's length. The hook is to stop the petals spinning around at the taping-up stage, though you might prefer not to create a hook.

12 Pinch the flowerpaste at the base down onto the wire. Place the petal onto the non-stick board and thin out the shape slightly using the non-stick rolling pin. Next, use the ceramic silk veining tool to roll the petal at intervals in a fan formation, creating a series of fine veins over the petal. Turn the petal over and repeat on the back. Use the same tool to create a gentle frill to the edge of the petal.

13 Hollow the centre of the petal using your fingers and thumb. Dry the petal in a homemade kitchen paper ring former. Repeat to make ten outer petals. The number varies but ten is a good starting point.

COLOURING AND ASSEMBLY

14 Mix together plum, edelweiss and a touch of African violet. Use a flat dusting brush to colour the petals from the base fading out towards the edges and then dust from the edges in towards the base. Repeat on the back of each petal.

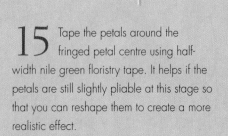

15 Tape the petals around the fringed petal centre using half-width nile green floristry tape. It helps if the petals are still slightly pliable at this stage so that you can reshape them to create a more realistic effect.

CALYX

16 There are three rounded sepals and two or three long leaf-like sepals that make up the calyx. The rounded sepals can be cut out using the three sizes of the standard rose petal cutter set or they can be made using a freehand technique, as illustrated here. Insert a 30- or 28-gauge

white wire into a ball of pale green flowerpaste. Work the base of the ball down onto the wire to form a cone shape. Flatten the shape against the non-stick board using the flat side of the single peony leaf veiner.

17 Next place the shape onto your palm and thin the edges using the metal ball tool. Hollow the shape too using the same tool. Pinch a slight point into the top edge. Repeat to make three sizes of sepal.

18 The longer leaf-like sepals are also made freehand. Roll a ball of pale green flowerpaste onto a 28-gauge white wire, blending the flowerpaste against the wire to form it into a long, slender leaf

shape pointed at both ends. Again, flatten the shape with the flat side of a leaf/petal veiner. Soften the edges and then pinch the shape from the base to the tip to create a central vein.

19 Dust each of the sepals with a mixture of foliage and vine petal dusts. Tinge the edges and tips with a mixture of aubergine and plum petal dusts. Spray lightly with edible spray varnish.

20 Use half-width nile green floristry tape to secure the three rounded sepals to the back of the flower with the hollowed-out side against the petals. Next,

add the longer leaf-like sepals in between the rounded sepals. These should fall away from the other sections of the calyx.

LEAVES

21 Roll out some well-kneaded mid-green flowerpaste, leaving a thick ridge for the wire – a grooved board can be used for this purpose.

22 Use the plain-edge cutting wheel to cut out a freehand leaf shape or use one of the cattleya orchid wing petal cutters if you prefer (these will need to be squashed slightly to create a longer, more slender shape).

23 Insert a 26- or 24-gauge white wire moistened with fresh egg white into the thick ridge of the leaf to support about half its length. Place the leaf onto the foam pad or the palm of your hand and soften the edges with the metal ball tool.

24 Place the leaf into the double-sided peony leaf veiner and press firmly to texture the leaf. Remove the leaf from the veiner and pinch it from the base through to the tip to accentuate the central vein. Repeat to make two smaller leaves to set on either side of the larger central leaf.

COLOURING

25 Dust the leaves in layers, starting with a very light dusting of forest petal dust. Over-dust heavily with foliage and then add some vine. Tinge the edges very slightly with aubergine petal dust. The backs of the leaves should be much paler in colour. Allow to dry and then spray lightly with edible spray varnish.

26 Tape the leaves together into sets of three using half-width nile green floristry tape.

Pink perfection spray

Fringed pink peonies combined with white tuberoses, blue-tinged medinilla berries and trailing piper foliage have been used here to create two very simple and yet stunning sprays of flowers, illustrating that you don't need huge quantities of flowers to create an impressive display.

MATERIALS

22-guage white wires

Teal green edible food spray (optional)

Nile green floristry tape

EQUIPMENT

Wire cutters or florist's scissors

Fine-nose pliers

Small white vase (optional)

FLOWERS

5 groups of medinilla berries (p 94)

6 trailing stems of piper foliage (p 136)

2 pink peonies, plus foliage (p 126)

6 stems of tuberoses (p 80)

PREPARATION

1 First, tape extra 22-gauge wire onto any of the flower and foliage stems that require extra support or length. Spray the medinilla berries with teal green edible food spray, but try to leave some of the original pink colour showing through. Leave to dry before using.

ASSEMBLY

2 Tape three stems of piper foliage around a single peony using half-width nile green floristry tape. Trim off any excess wires using wire cutters or florist's scissors. Curve the trailing stems a little as you work using fine-nose pliers. The trails of foliage should form a lazy 'S' shape for the spray used on the top tier; the bottom spray has a more relaxed curved shape.

3 Next, add the stems of tuberoses following the line created by the trailing foliage. Add the peony leaves to fill in more of the space around the peony flower.

4 Finally add the medinilla berries, positioning them evenly around the edges of the spray. Repeat to make second spray and display both sprays on a cake, or as illustrated here, in a small white ceramic vase.

Orchid trail wedding

An informal trailing bouquet of tropical fringed vanda orchids adorns this wedding cake. A silver candle holder with a flat base makes an unusual and yet perfect separator for this attractive two-tier cake.

MATERIALS

15 cm (6 in) and 23 cm (9 in) round fruitcakes placed on thin cake boards of the same size

1.4 kg (3 lb 2 oz) white almond paste

1.8 kg (4 lb) pink sugarpaste

33 cm (13 in) round cake drum

Pink organza ribbon

Clear alcohol (Cointreau or kirsch)

Plum satin ribbon

Non-toxic glue stick

Cocoa butter, grated

Mug and saucer

Foliage, edelweiss, vine and plum petal dusts

EQUIPMENT

Straight-edged sugarpaste smoother

Assorted paintbrushes

Silver candle holder

3 food-grade plastic dowels (optional)

Food-grade plastic posy pick

Fine-nose pliers

FLOWERS

Orchid trail bouquet (p 138)

PREPARATION

1 Cover the cakes and cake drum as described on pages 11–12. Allow to dry overnight. Place the larger cake on top of the cake drum and use the straight-edged sugarpaste smoother to blend the join between the cake and the board. Attach a band of pink organza ribbon around the base of each cake, using a little sugarpaste softened with clear alcohol to secure it in place at the back. Secure the plum satin ribbon to the cake drum's edge using non-toxic glue.

SIDE DESIGN

2 Melt some grated cocoa butter onto a saucer above a mug filled with just-boiled water. Mix in a small amount of foliage, edelweiss and vine petal dusts to form an opaque paint. Use a fine paintbrush to paint a trailing stem of pointed leaves onto the top of the bottom tier, trailing slightly onto the side. Allow to set before adding more foliage petal dust to the melted mixture and then add an outline and shading to each leaf. Mix up a separate amount of melted cocoa butter and add some plum petal dust with a touch of edelweiss. Paint a series of dotted trailing flowers at intervals in the leaf design.

ASSEMBLY

3 Place the silver candle holder on top of the bottom tier. You might prefer to cut three plastic dowels the depth of the coated cake and insert them into the cake in the area that the candle holder is to be positioned to add extra support to the tiered cake. Place the smaller cake on top of the candle holder. Insert the posy pick into the top tier.

4 Assemble the trailing orchid bouquet, then insert the handle of the bouquet into the posy pick. Use fine-nose pliers to curl and bend any of the components in the bouquet so that they sit well with the position of the two cakes.

Pink-fringed vanda orchid

This unusual orchid is actually part of the *Vanda* orchid family – with an added dash of my own artistic licence. Most *Vanda* orchids have quite round, flat-faced flowers. I like the split-fringed lip of this variety, which has more interest and drama than some of the more familiar varieties.

FRINGED LABELLUM/LIP

1 Squash the smallest cutter from the simple leaf cutter set to make a more curved shape (or see the simple leaf template on page 140). Roll out some well-kneaded white flowerpaste, leaving a fine ridge for the wire. Cut out the shape using the squashed cutter. Insert a 30-gauge white wire moistened with fresh egg white into the ridge to support about half the length of the petal. Pinch the base of the petal onto the wire and work it between your finger and thumb to create an elongated fine section.

2 Place the petal against the non-stick board and use the broad end of the dresden tool to thin out and frill the edge – this technique is known as 'double frilling'. Work the edge of the petal at intervals around petal. Next, place the petal into the double-sided stargazer B petal veiner and press firmly to texture the petal.

3 Rest the petal against your finger and vein the edges slightly using the ceramic silk veining tool to roll against the flowerpaste. Next, cut into the edge of the petal using a pair of fine scissors and create a fringed effect, removing the occasional slender 'V'-shape.

4 Pinch the petal from the base to the tip and flick the fringe a little to give more movement. Repeat to make a second petal, turning the cutter over to create a mirror image. Tape the two petals together using quarter-width white floristry tape.

5 The next section of the labellum is quite fleshy. Take a ball of white flowerpaste and wrap it around where the two petals meet. Work the flowerpaste down the wire to a length of between 3.5–5 cm (1½–2 in) long. The flowerpaste should be finer where the two petals meet and broader at the base. Next, flatten the length of this section and pinch out two flanges on either side. Place the shape onto the foam pad and using the small metal ball tool, thin the edges and hollow them.

6 Use a pair of fine-angle tweezers to pinch three ridges down the length of the thick section of flowerpaste. Pinch the two hollowed flange sections from behind to heighten their position. Curve the thicker length of the petal. Leave to dry slightly before colouring.

COLUMN

7 Attach a small ball of white flowerpaste to the end of a 26-gauge white wire. Thin the base to form a cone shape. Hollow

MATERIALS

White and pale green flowerpaste

30-, 28- and 26-gauge white wires

Fresh egg white

White floristry tape

Plum, African violet, sunflower, daffodil, edelweiss, foliage, vine and aubergine petal dusts

Isopropyl alcohol

EQUIPMENT

Simple leaf cutters (TT)

Non-stick rolling pin

Non-stick board

Dresden tool

Stargazer B petal veiner

Ceramic silk veining tool

Fine scissors

Foam pad

Small metal ball tool

Fine-angled tweezers

Dusting brushes

Fine paintbrushes

out the underside of the column using the rounded end of the ceramic silk veining tool. Pinch a subtle ridge down the back of the column. Attach a tiny ball of white flowerpaste to the tip. Divide into two sections down the length of the ball. Allow to dry and then tape onto the base of the fringed labellum using quarter-width white floristry tape.

COLOURING

8 Dust the fringed petals heavily with plum petal dust. Continue the colour down onto the thick ridged area and catch the edges of the hollowed-out flanged sections. Add a touch of African violet. Dilute some plum and African violet petal dusts with isopropyl alcohol to paint the ridged sections. Dust the area at the centre of the hollowed flanged area with a mixture of sunflower and daffodil mixed together.

OUTER SEPALS (DORSAL AND LATERAL)

9 There are three outer sepals – a head (dorsal) and two legs (lateral sepals). Roll out some white flowerpaste, leaving a thick ridge for the wire. Cut out the sepal shape using the larger squashed simple leaf cutter (or see the simple leaf template on page 140). Insert a 28-gauge white wire moistened with fresh egg white into the sepal to support about a third of the length.

10 Soften the edge of the sepal and then place it into the double-sided stargazer B petal veiner to texture. Remove the sepal from the veiner and pinch gently from the base through to the tip to accentuate the central vein. Curve back slightly. Repeat the process to create two lateral sepals (legs), curving them to create a bow-legged finish.

LATERAL PETALS

11 These are made in the same way as the outer sepals, but once the shape is cut out use the same cutter repositioned on the edge to re-cut, making the petal slightly narrower in shape. Repeat to make a left and right petal.

ASSEMBLY AND COLOURING

12 Tape the two lateral petals onto either side of the column using quarter-width white floristry tape. Position and tape in the dorsal sepal behind the lateral petals to fill the space in between. Add the lateral sepals at the base of the flower. Dust the petals and outer sepals using a mixture of plum, African violet and edelweiss petal dusts. Start the colour at the base of each petal/sepal and fade it out towards the edges. Dust the backs in the same way.

13 Dilute some plum, African violet and edelweiss petal dusts with isopropyl alcohol to form a painting medium. Use a fine paintbrush to add spots at the base, fading towards mid-way on each petal/sepal.

OVARY

14 Add a fine sausage of pale green flowerpaste behind the outer sepals and thin it down to create a slender ovary. Use the plain-edge cutting wheel to add fine lines down the length of the ovary. Curve slightly. Dust with a mixture of foliage and vine petal dusts. Add a tinge of aubergine just behind the base of the outer sepals and also at the base of the ovary. Steam to set the colour and take away the dry dusted finish.

Piper

There are over 2,000 tropical species of piper, with *Piper nigrum* being the most important source of pepper – reputed to be the oldest trade between the Orient and Europe. If the berries are collected and dried before they ripen, the result is black peppercorns. If the black casing is removed by maceration, the berries yield white pepper. The piper illustrated here is based on a more ornamental species. The pink veins fade to white as the leaves mature.

MATERIALS

Mid-green flowerpaste

28-, 26-, 24- and 22-gauge white wires

Fresh egg white

Nile green floristry tape

Woodland, foliage, aubergine and plum petal dusts

White bridal satin dust

Isopropyl alcohol

Edible spray varnish

EQUIPMENT

Non-stick rolling pin

Plain-edge cutting wheel

Foam pad

Medium metal ball tool

Single peony leaf veiner (SKGI)

Dusting brushes

Fine paintbrush

LEAVES

1 Roll out some well-kneaded mid-green flowerpaste, leaving a thick ridge for the wire. Use the plain-edge cutting wheel to cut out a freehand leaf shape that is quite rounded at the base with a tapered point.

2 Insert a 28-, 26- or 24-gauge white wire moistened with fresh egg white into the thick ridge to support about half the length of the leaf. The gauge of the wire will depend on the size of the leaf you are making.

3 Soften the edge of the leaf, working half on the flowerpaste and half on your hand/foam pad with the medium metal ball tool. Next, texture the leaf using the double-sided single peony leaf veiner. Remove the leaf from the veiner and pinch it from the base through to the tip to accentuate the central vein and curve the tip of the leaf slightly. Repeat to make leaves in graduating sizes. Tape over each leaf stem with quarter-width nile green floristry tape.

COLOURING AND ASSEMBLY

4 Dust the leaves in layers with woodland and then foliage petal dusts. Catch the edges very gently with aubergine petal dust.

5 Dilute some white bridal satin dust with isopropyl alcohol and add a touch of plum petal dust. Use a fine paintbrush to paint a series of veins onto each leaf. Try not to be too precise with this process – it helps to create an almost dotted line with each vein. Allow to dry. If the paintwork looks too severe, carefully over-dust gently with a little more foliage petal dust. Allow to dry and then spray lightly with edible spray varnish.

6 Use a small leaf on the end of a 24-gauge white wire, taping it in place with half-width nile green floristry tape. Continue adding the leaves down the stem, gradually increasing the size as you work. For longer stems, add an extra 22-gauge white wire to give more support. Curve and bend the leaves and the main stem to create more movement. Dust the stems with foliage and a little aubergine petal dusts.

Cordyline

These highly coloured and decorative cordyline leaves add an instant touch of the exotic to any bouquet or arrangement. This plant has many common names, but my favourite is the Good Luck plant. There are several variations but I have chosen a form with bright pink leaves and dark aubergine markings. There are cream varieties with pink and green stripes, pale pink forms and even coppery coloured ones, too.

NEW GROWTH

1 At the top of the plant there is usually one unfurling leaf. Roll out some well-kneaded pink flowerpaste, leaving a thick ridge for the wire. Cut out a basic leaf shape freehand, using the large end of the plain-edge cutting wheel. Alternatively, you might prefer to use the simple leaf template on page 140.

2 Insert a 26-gauge white wire moistened with fresh egg white into the leaf to support about half its length. Work the base of the leaf down onto the wire to create a thickened stem. Place the leaf on the foam pad and soften the edges with the large metal ball tool.

3 Place the leaf into the double-sided large tulip leaf veiner and firmly press to texture the surface. Remove the leaf from the veiner and place it back onto the foam pad. Use the fine end of the plain-edge cutting wheel to draw a central vein down the leaf. Next, pinch the leaf from the base to the tip to accentuate the central vein and give more shape.

4 Apply a small amount of fresh egg white to the base of one edge of the leaf and then roll it up slightly to create the impression of an unfurling leaf. Repeat the process to create larger, flatter foliage in graduating sizes. Use 24- and 22-gauge white wires for the larger leaves.

COLOURING

5 Dust the leaves back and front with plum petal dust. Dilute some aubergine petal dust with isopropyl alcohol and paint fine central veins on the smaller leaves, and heavier brushstrokes on the backs and fronts of the larger, more mature leaves. Catch the very edge of the leaf with this diluted colour too. Allow to dry and then over-dust the painted areas with aubergine petal dust. Add a touch of foliage petal dust to the smaller leaves too. Allow to dry and then spray with edible spray varnish.

MATERIALS

Pink flowerpaste
26-, 24- and 22-gauge white wires
Fresh egg white
Plum, aubergine and foliage petal dusts
Isopropyl alcohol
Edible spray varnish

EQUIPMENT

Non-stick rolling pin
Plain-edge cutting wheel
Foam pad
Large metal ball tool
Large tulip leaf veiner (SKGI)
Dusting brushes
Fine paintbrush

Orchid trail bouquet

Unusual pink-fringed vanda orchids are used as the focal flower in this trailing exotic bouquet. I love creating tangled and interesting-shaped bouquets; here trails of pink metallic wire and pink and purple decorative paper-covered wires help to create an interesting freestyle display.

MATERIALS

Nile green floristry tape
22-gauge white wires
Silver, pink and purple paper-covered florist's wires
Pink metallic florist's wire

EQUIPMENT

Tape shredder or scissors
Fine-nose pliers
Wire cutters or heavy-duty florist's scissors
Glass vase

FLOWERS

3 pink-fringed vanda orchids (p 134)
3 begonia leaves (p 112)
5 trails of piper foliage (p 136)
5 pink cordyline leaves (p 137)
3 sprigs of medinilla berries (p 94)
5 groups of king tillandsia foliage (p 103)

PREPARATION

1 Cut several lengths of half-width nile green floristry tape using a tape shredder or a pair of scissors. Strengthen any flower or foliage stems that require extra support by taping them onto 22-gauge white wires.

ASSEMBLY

2 Form the basic framework for the bouquet using the silver paper-covered florist's wire to create a tangled ball, which will sit at the centre of the bouquet. Tape two lengths of pink metallic florist's wire through the tangled ball using half-width nile green floristry tape to hold them together and form a handle. Use fine-nose pliers to re-adjust the position and curve, and bend the wires into shape.

3 Pull in two pink-fringed vanda orchids to create the focal point of the bouquet. Add a couple of begonia leaves to frame the flowers. Trim off any excess wires as you work to keep the handle fairly slim.

4 Add two long trails of piper foliage to follow the lines of the metallic wires and bulk out the focal area using three pink cordyline leaves.

5 Continue adding extra pieces of plant material – the three sprigs of medinilla berries, some tillandsia foliage and a few extra short pieces of piper foliage.

6 Next add the third orchid, accompanied by a couple of cordyline leaves and a group of tillandsia onto the tail end of the pink metallic wires using nile green floristry tape, which will then be covered with a few pieces of coloured paper-covered wires to bind it into the display. Complete the bouquet using a few trails of pink, purple and silver paper-covered florist's wires to snake through the whole length of the bouquet. Display the bouquet in a pretty glass vase.

2

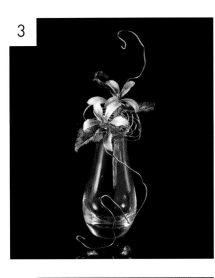

3

4

5

TEMPLATES

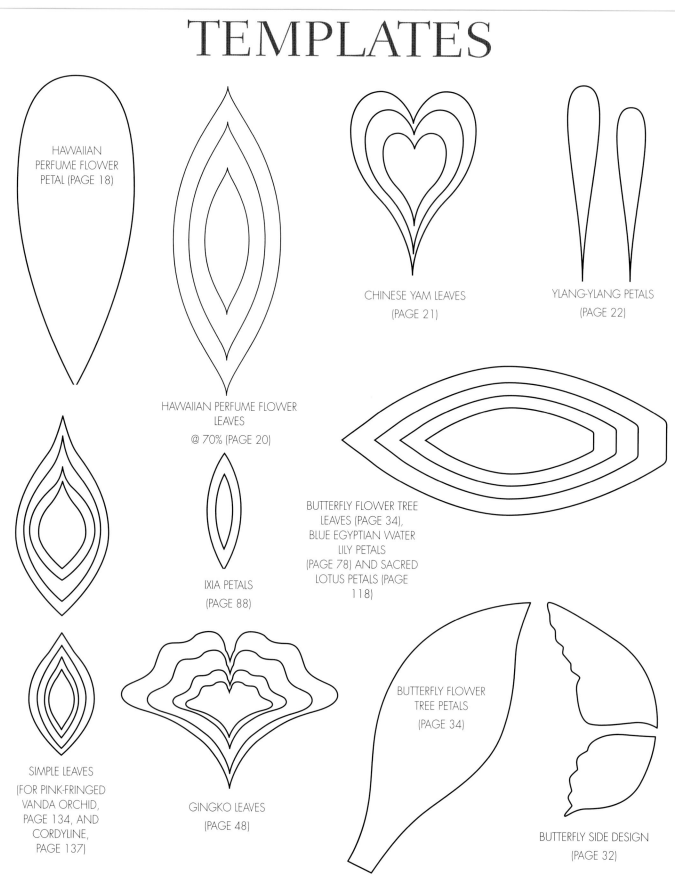

HAWAIIAN
PERFUME FLOWER
PETAL (PAGE 18)

HAWAIIAN PERFUME FLOWER
LEAVES
@ 70% (PAGE 20)

CHINESE YAM LEAVES
(PAGE 21)

YLANG-YLANG PETALS
(PAGE 22)

IXIA PETALS
(PAGE 88)

BUTTERFLY FLOWER TREE
LEAVES (PAGE 34),
BLUE EGYPTIAN WATER
LILY PETALS
(PAGE 78) AND SACRED
LOTUS PETALS (PAGE
118)

SIMPLE LEAVES
(FOR PINK-FRINGED
VANDA ORCHID,
PAGE 134, AND
CORDYLINE,
PAGE 137)

GINGKO LEAVES
(PAGE 48)

BUTTERFLY FLOWER
TREE PETALS
(PAGE 34)

BUTTERFLY SIDE DESIGN
(PAGE 32)

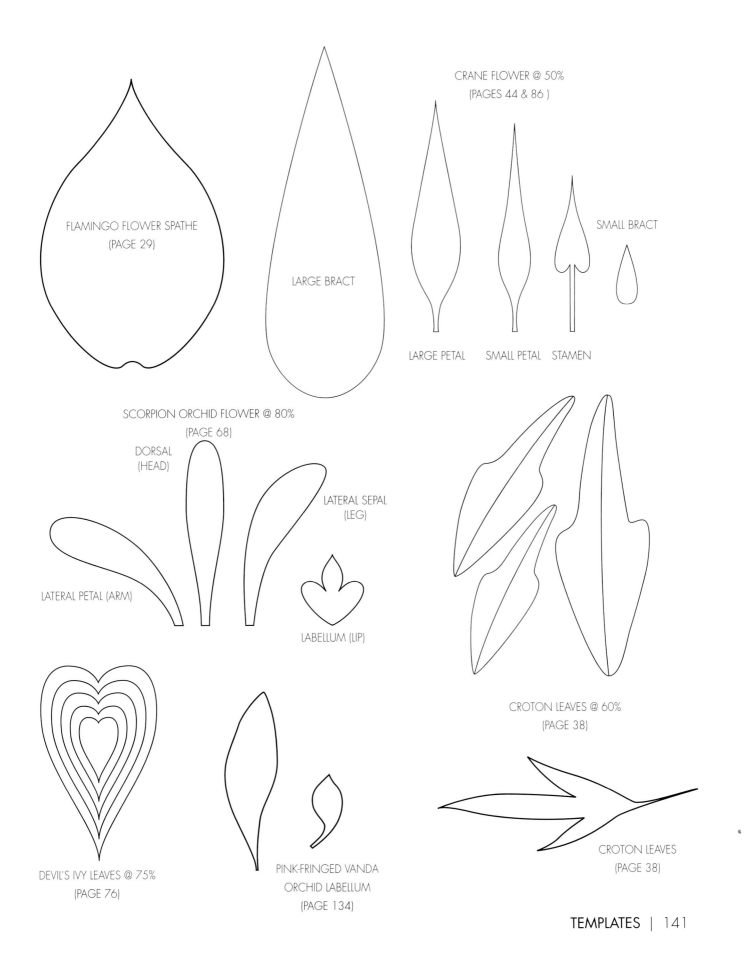

FLAMINGO FLOWER SPATHE
(PAGE 29)

LARGE BRACT

CRANE FLOWER @ 50%
(PAGES 44 & 86)

SMALL BRACT

LARGE PETAL   SMALL PETAL   STAMEN

SCORPION ORCHID FLOWER @ 80%
(PAGE 68)

DORSAL
(HEAD)

LATERAL SEPAL
(LEG)

LATERAL PETAL (ARM)

LABELLUM (LIP)

CROTON LEAVES @ 60%
(PAGE 38)

DEVIL'S IVY LEAVES @ 75%
(PAGE 76)

PINK-FRINGED VANDA
ORCHID LABELLUM
(PAGE 134)

CROTON LEAVES
(PAGE 38)

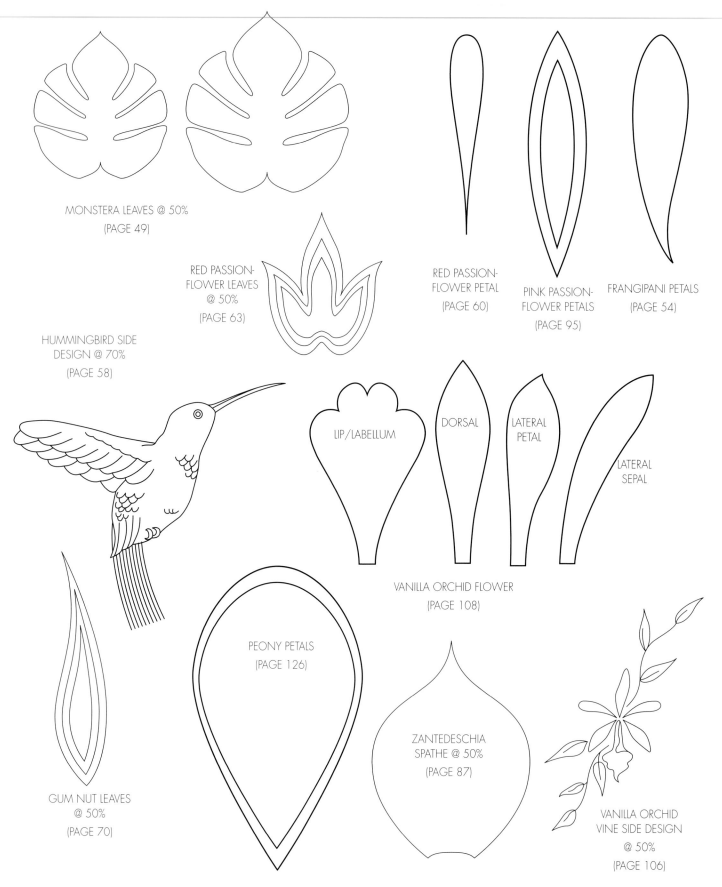

MONSTERA LEAVES @ 50%
(PAGE 49)

RED PASSION-
FLOWER LEAVES
@ 50%
(PAGE 63)

HUMMINGBIRD SIDE
DESIGN @ 70%
(PAGE 58)

RED PASSION-
FLOWER PETAL
(PAGE 60)

PINK PASSION-
FLOWER PETALS
(PAGE 95)

FRANGIPANI PETALS
(PAGE 54)

LIP/LABELLUM

DORSAL

LATERAL
PETAL

LATERAL
SEPAL

VANILLA ORCHID FLOWER
(PAGE 108)

PEONY PETALS
(PAGE 126)

GUM NUT LEAVES
@ 50%
(PAGE 70)

ZANTEDESCHIA
SPATHE @ 50%
(PAGE 87)

VANILLA ORCHID
VINE SIDE DESIGN
@ 50%
(PAGE 106)

LIST OF SUPPLIERS

A PIECE OF CAKE (APOC)
18 Upper High Street
Thame
Oxon OX9 3EX
01844 213428
www.sugaricing.com

ALDAVAL VEINERS (ALDV)
16 Chibburn Court
Widdrington
Morpeth
Northumberland NE61 5QT
+44 (0)1670 790 995

CAKES, CLASSES AND CUTTERS
23 Princes Road
Brunton Park
Gosforth
Newcastle-upon-Tyne NE3 5TT
www.cakesclassesandcutters.co.uk

CELCAKES AND CELCRAFTS (CC)
Springfield House
Gate Helmsley
York YO4 1NF
www.celcrafts.co.uk

CELEBRATIONS
Unit 383 G
Jedburgh Court
Team Valley Trading Estate
Gateshead
Tyne and Wear NE11 0BQ
www.celebrations-teamvalley.co.uk

CULPITT CAKE ART
Jubilee Industrial Estate
Ashington
Northumberland NE63 8UG
www.culpitt.com

DESIGN-A-CAKE
30/31 Phoenix Road
Crowther Industrial Estate
Washington
Tyne & Wear NE38 0AD
www.design-a-cake.co.uk

GUY, PAUL & CO LTD
(UK distributor for Jem cutters)
Unit 10 The Business Centre
Corinium Industrial estate
Raans Road
Amersham
Buckinghamshire HP6 6FB
www.guypaul.co.uk

HOLLY PRODUCTS (HP)
Primrose Cottage
Church Walk
Norton in Hales
Shropshire TF9 4QX
www.hollyproducts.co.uk

ITEMS FOR SUGARCRAFT
72 Godstone Road
Kenley
Surrey CR8 5AA
www.itemsforsugarcraft.co.uk

ORCHARD PRODUCTS (OPR)
51 Hallyburton Road
Hove, East Sussex BN3 7GP
www.orchardproducts.co.uk

THE BRITISH SUGARCRAFT GUILD
for more information contact:
Wellington House
Messeter Place
Eltham
London SE9 5DP
www.bsguk.org

THE OLD BAKERY
Kingston St Mary
Taunton
Somerset TA2 8HW
www.oldbakery.co.uk

TINKERTECH TWO (TT)
40 Langdon Road
Parkstone
Poole
Dorset BH14 9EH

SQUIRES KITCHEN (SKGI)
Squires House
3 Waverley Lane
Farnham
Surrey GU9 8BB
www.squires-shop.com

AUSTRALIA
My Cake Delights
219 High Street
Preston 3072
Melbourne
www.mycakedelights.com

Contact the author
www.alandunnsugarcraft.com

INDEX